COMPETENCY TO STAND TRIAL:

DEVELOPMENT AND CURRENT STATUS

E. Basil Jackson
M.D., J.D., D.Litt., Ph.D.

GlobalEdAdvance
Press

COMPETENCY TO STAND TRIAL

Development and Current Status

Copyright © 2013 by E. Basil Jackson

Library of Congress Control Number: 2012956367

COMPETENCY TO STAND TRIAL

ISBN 978-1-935434-15-3

Subject Codes and Description: 1. Law:041000: Law: Forensic Science; 2. Law 003000: Law: Alternative Dispute Resolution; 3. Law 060000: Law: Legal History.

Cover Design by Brian Lane Green

Printed in Australia, Brazil, France, Germany, Italy, Spain, UK, and USA.

The Press does not have ownership of the contents of a book; this is the author's work and the author owns the copyright. All theory, concepts, constructs, and perspectives are those of the author and not necessarily the Press. They are presented for open and free discussion of the issues involved. All comments and feedback should be directed to the Email: [*comments4author@aol.com*] and the comments will be forwarded to the author for response.

Published by

GlobalEdAdvance Press

www.gea-books.com

Dedication

Lovingly dedicated to

Lorraine Jackson M.D.

"A Gift from the Lord"

CONTENTS

Lex plus laudatur quando ratione probatur.

~

**The law is to receive more approbation
when it is consistent with reason.**

FOREWORD

Whether it is a highly publicized homicide or other serious criminal case, inexplicably committed by a person with no prior criminal history but some mental health concerns, or a defendant who stops taking his psychotropic medications and runs afoul of the criminal law, or an offender who is not competent to understand the trial process or assist his/her attorney, the psychiatrist and psychologist have become an integral part of court proceedings and the American criminal justice system. Experienced criminal defense attorneys frequently consult with psychiatrists to determine whether their client's symptomology, behavior and state of mind rises to the level required for presentation of a plausible insanity defense. Problems with a defendant's competency to proceed in court is a frequent precursor to many potential insanity defense cases and can be either a mitigating or aggravating factor at trial and sentencing regardless.

Dr. Basil Jackson has been a practicing psychiatrist in Wisconsin for over fifty years, and his professional services have been utilized in all varieties of criminal cases by the defense and prosecution and his opinions relied upon by courts. Dr. Jackson is a recognized expert in examining criminal defendants for purposes of not guilty by reason of mental disease (insanity defense) assessments and competency to proceed to trial and assist counsel determinations. Dr. Jackson has consulted in or been deposed or testified in court in hundreds of cases in Wisconsin, the United States and overseas.

My law firm and I have retained and utilized Dr. Jackson's services in a number of criminal cases over the past three decades. His insights and opinions as a forensic expert have helped us immensely in determining what kind of mental problems our clients suffer from and whether that mental condition impacted the client's ability to perceive and understand the proceedings and assist defense counsel, to differentiate between right and wrong (the M'Naghten Rule) or to conform his conduct to the requirements of the law (from the ALI Model Penal Code).

From his years of experience in forensic psychiatry, Dr. Jackson has written a text that details not only the legal and medical concerns surrounding the competency to stand trial issue, but highlights the ethical and moral considerations that underlie our system of assessing competence and personal responsibility, when the common presumptions regarding understanding, intent and responsibility for one's actions are called into serious question because of mental illness or disability.

The issue of competency in our criminal justice system is whether a defendant is able to adequately assist his attorney in preparing a defense, make informed decisions about trial strategy and whether or not to plead guilty, accept a plea agreement or go to trial. Competency largely deals with the defendant's present condition, while criminal responsibility addresses the condition at the time the crime was committed. Dr. Jackson presents representative case histories which help to illuminate the legal, ethical and moral conflicts and dangers inherent in having a psychiatrist or psychologist opine whether a defendant who is medicated back to a level of competence can or should go forward to trial, predicting future competence and conduct, and the considerations as to when a defendant should be absolved from a penal consequence based on mental incompetence.

Dr. Jackson's insights draws on many disciplines as he challenges many of the assumptions that those of us who "labor in the vineyard" of the criminal justice system take for granted and consider as being the appropriate norm. He gives us pause to reflect on the continued viability and societal consequences of commonly accepted principles in our day-to-day practice.

Raymond M. Dall'Osto, Attorney

Gimbel, Reilly, Guerin & Brown LLP

Milwaukee, Wisconsin 53202

§

"...Then saith he unto them, Render therefore unto Caesar the things that are Caesar's; and unto God the things that are God's." [1]

INTRODUCTION

For well over two thousand years, Western civilization has made a judgment that the mentally ill suffer not only from an illness, but also from a social condition.[2] Nor has it been alone in this judgment; indeed, this view is almost uniform throughout the world.[3] The result of this judgment is that the mentally ill have for a long time been held not responsible for their actions, be they of a civil or criminal nature.[4] Certain problems accompany such a decision. Society needs to distinguish the severely mentally ill, from those who may be ill but not severely. A decision needs to be made about what to do with the mentally ill, in lieu of legal liability. Society has grappled with these questions for generations, with each generation purportedly giving a more progressive and humane answer.

Development Of Competency To Stand Trial

As the science of medicine in general and of psychiatry[5] in particular has developed, the criminal justice system has attempted to harvest the increased scientific knowledge so that it could help in answering these questions (although it has remained somewhat ambivalent about psychiatric involvement).[6] Psychiatrists are now closely involved in multiple stages of criminal justice administration.[7] Such involvement has quite often been lauded as it is perceived to be scientific, and thus objective, ridding the criminal justice system of arbitrariness and uncertainty in its involvement with the criminally insane.[8] Today psychiatrists are involved in every stage of the criminal process, from the preliminary hearing to long after conviction or acquittal by reason of insanity.[9] Because of their undisputed expertise in mental health, some of the judgments that psychiatrists make go unquestioned by the criminal justice system.[10] When such judgments are questioned however, a "battle of the experts" ensues[11] where the scientific truth gets lost.[12]

Psychiatrists are often asked to testify on issues that they have no particular expertise in. A psychiatrist cannot intelligently answer whether the accused poses future danger, yet such questions are routinely asked. A psychiatrist also has no specialized knowledge to answer such questions of morality as "did the person know 'right from wrong' or 'good from evil." However, the courts do tend to allow psychiatrists to offer testimony on such essentially moral questions. Thus, psychiatrists are tempted to justify the judgments of the courts or alternatively to substitute their own morality for that of the rest of the society (as expressed by the jury). Such intertwining of medicine and the law does not do justice, and reflects poorly on the medical profession. The "battle of the experts" and the resultant and concomitant distrust that lay juries often end up having in experts[13] are but a symptom of this problem. This review argues that despite the benefits of ridding the criminal justice system of some uncertainty and ignorance with respect to mental health issues, the very close involvement of psychiatrists in the criminal justice system as practiced in the United States is not only illogical and bad policy, but also unethical from the viewpoint of medical ethics.

Part II of this review will lay the groundwork for the argument by discussing the history of the insanity defense, and of science's involvement with criminal justice; while Part III, will look into the association of science and the administration of justice in the modern world. Part IV will argue that the alternative methods of linking psychiatry and the criminal justice system, such as independent expert panels, do not solve the fundamental problem of psychiatrists working beyond their ethical boundaries. Finally, Part V will focus on the ethical principles that should guide a psychiatrist in his involvement with the judiciary.

1. The issue of competency to stand trial is one of the most important but misunderstood issues in the interface between the mental health professions and the criminal justice process. It is an important issue because it is raised in far more cases than is the insanity defense and results in four times as many criminal defendants being confined for treatment than does the insanity defense. Nevertheless, it is a misunderstood issue because it is often confused with the insanity defense. Incompetency to stand trial sometimes referred to as "present insanity," focuses on the defendant's ability to under- stand the criminal trial process that he or she is undergoing and to assist the defense attorney in defending against the criminal charge. The insanity defense sometimes referred to as "past insanity," focuses on the defendant's mental state at the time of the alleged crime and asks whether the defendant should be absolved from criminal responsibility. Although the two issues focus on the defendant's mental state at different times and for different purposes, nevertheless Ronald Roesch and Stephen Golding report: [B]oth law and psychiatry continue to confuse the two standards and

to apply indiscriminately the mental health criteria for responsibility to competency standards. In both cases mental health professionals in general and psychiatrists in particular, continue to exhibit a marked tendency to equate psychosis with responsibility and/or competency, in spite of the fact that this is not in accord with either legal standard.

If a defendant is suspected of being incompetent to stand trial, the criminal proceedings are suspended until the defendant is evaluated and determined to be competent or, if found incompetent, until the defendant has been restored to competency. The American Bar Foundation has suggested that the suspension of the criminal proceedings is warranted in order to assure the accuracy, fairness, and dignity of the trial process and to justify the imposition of punishment if the defendant is convicted.[14] In many cases, the accused may be the only individual who has knowledge of the facts underlying the criminal charge; thus, an accurate assessment of guilt requires the defendant's assistance. To assure fairness in the criminal process, the accused must have the basic capacity to assist counsel in presenting a defense. The dignity of the criminal process would be undermined by the spectacle of an incompetent defendant's trial. The objective of punishment requires that a convicted defendant comprehend the reasons why punishment is being imposed.

In Drope v. Missouri,[15] the United States Supreme Court ruled that the prohibition against conducting a criminal trial of an incompetent defendant "is fundamental to an adversary system of justice."[16] To assure that an incompetent defendant is not deprived of the due process right to a fair trial, the court, the prosecutor, and the defense attorney all have an obligation to raise the issue whenever reasonable cause exists to believe that the accused is incompetent. Thus, in Pate v. Robinson,[17] the Supreme Court ruled that notwithstanding the defendant's mental alertness and understanding as displayed by his conversations with the trial judge, a hearing on the defendant's competence to stand trial was required because of the un-contradicted testimony of the defendant's history of pronounced irrational behavior. At the hearing, the defendant's demeanor at trial might well be relevant to determining whether the defendant was presently competent, but the defendant's demeanor could not be relied upon to dispense with the necessity of holding a hearing on the issue altogether. In Drope, the Supreme Court stated that the import of the Pate v. Robinson decision "is that evidence of a defendant's irrational behavior, his demeanor at trial, and any prior medical opinion on competence to stand trial are all relevant in determining whether further inquiry is required, but that even one of these factors standing alone may, in some circumstances, be sufficient."[18] Indeed, one author has suggested that trial judges, wishing to avoid possible reversals, will order competency evaluations for virtually every criminal defendant who appears to be mentally ill at any time during the criminal proceedings.

The Pate standard was criticized by Professors Roesch and Golding as "problematical" because a liberal application results in an overuse of competency hearings while a conservative interpretation results in the denial of a defendant's due process rights. The authors commended courts that weigh the evidence from a functional perspective. Thus, in People v. Laudermilk, the California Supreme Court noted that "more is required to raise a doubt than mere bizarre actions . . . or bizarre statements . . . or statements of defense counsel that the defendant is incapable of cooperating in his defense . . . or psychiatric testimony that the defendant is immature, dangerous, psychopathic, or homicidal or such diagnosis with little reference to the defendant's ability to assist in his own defense. . . ."

In one recent case, defense counsel requested a competency hearing. At the hearing, the request was withdrawn, but the defendant made a motion seeking transfer from the jail in which he had been incarcerated since his arrest. To support his request, the defendant personally related bizarre incidents of mistreatment in the jail, including assertions that heroin had been injected into his birthmarks and moles and that he had been raped while he was drugged.[19] The trial court denied the motion for jail transfer, and the case proceeded to trial. The United States Court of Appeals for the Ninth Circuit ruled that the defendant was not entitled to a pretrial competency hearing.

Even though the court characterized the defendant's beliefs as "undeniably weird,"[20] no evidence was presented to establish that his beliefs affected his ability to assist in the defense of his case.

If substantial evidence raises a doubt in the mind of the trial judge as to the defendant's mental competence, the judge is required to order a competency hearing notwithstanding the existence of other persuasive evidence of the defendant's competence, including testimony of witnesses or the court's own observations of the accused. [21] Because due process requires a competent defendant, the issue of the defendant's competency to stand trial is not a matter of trial tactics. Thus, once the issue is raised, the defendant may not choose to waive the hearing and proceed directly to trial.

2. In Dusky v. United States,[22] a 1960 per curiam decision of the United States Supreme Court, the Court announced a test of competency to stand trial that is used in federal prosecutions and, with little variation, in a majority of states. Quoting approvingly from the brief submitted by the Solicitor General, the Court ruled that the test of competency to stand trial "must be whether [defendant] has sufficient present ability to consult with his lawyer with a reasonable degree of rational understanding--and whether he has a rational as well as factual understanding of the proceedings against him."[23] Although the Court noted that competency to stand trial requires more than a finding that the defendant is oriented to time and place and has some recollection of events, the Court offered no further guidance on how to construe the language of the Dusky test. The Honorable John Oliver, a United States District Court judge whose district includes the federal institution to which many criminal defendants are sent for evaluations of their competency to stand trial, asserted that the Dusky opinion was "somewhat cryptic."[24] He added: "No one quarrels with what the Supreme Court actually held in Dusky; unhappiness with Dusky is produced by the fact that the Supreme Court said so little as to why it held what it did."[25]

In Wieter v. Settle,[26] Judge Oliver focused on the two components of the Dusky test: the defendant's capacity to understand the criminal process and the defendant's ability to function in that process. He asserted that a defendant should be found competent to stand trial if it is proven (1) that he has mental capacity to appreciate his presence in relation to time, place, and things; (2) that his elementary mental processes are such that he apprehends (i.e., seizes and grasps with what mind he has) that he is in a Court of Justice, charged with a criminal offense; (3) that there is a Judge on the Bench; (4) a Prosecutor present who will try to convict him of a criminal charge; (5) that he has a lawyer (self-employed or Court-appointed) who will undertake to defend him against that charge; (6) that he will be expected to tell his lawyer the circumstances, to the best of his mental ability, (whether colored or not by mental aberration) the facts surrounding him at the time and place where the law violation is alleged to have been committed; (7) that there is, or will be, a jury present to pass upon evidence adduced as to his guilt or innocence of such charge; and (8) he has memory sufficient to relate those things in his own personal manner. . . . [27]

In applying the Dusky test, federal courts have ruled consistently that mental illness, in and of itself, should not be equated to incompetence to stand trial.[28] Merely because a defendant is diagnosed as suffering from paranoia[29] or paranoid schizophrenia[30] does not mean that he or she is unable to understand the criminal charges and to assist in the defense. Even if the defendant is likely to lose composure or even break down under questioning and cry, he or she may be found competent if this conduct can be controlled so that it does not interfere substantially with the proper conduct of the proceedings. Thus, in United States v. Horowitz,[31] a defendant who was subject to such outbursts was found competent because his disruptions ended within a few minutes after he was taken from the courtroom.

3. That portion of the Dusky test requiring the defendant to have "sufficient present ability to consult with his or her attorney with a reasonable degree of rational understanding" has been subject to varying interpretations.

In Wieter v. Settle,[32] only one part of Judge Oliver's eight-part formula embellishing the Dusky test was devoted specifically to the issue of the defendant's ability to consult with his or her attorney. According to Judge Oliver, the defendant must understand that he or she is expected to inform the defense attorney of the circumstances and the facts surrounding the defendant at the time and place of the alleged law violation.[33] Other federal courts have also stressed defendants' ability to inform their attorneys of the facts and names of witnesses because defendants usually assist in this phase of a defense and not in legal questions involved in the defense. As Judge Oliver noted in United States v. Sermon,[34] "Defendants do not assist in their own defense by telling their lawyers what motions to file or how a particular witness should be examined or cross-examined. . . . [T]he primary assistance that must be rendered counsel is a full revelation of the facts within the knowledge of the defendant in areas which are in legitimate dispute."[35]

Other courts, however, require more of a defendant than a mere ability to recite the facts surrounding the alleged crime. These courts focus on the defendant's ability to participate effectively in pretrial decision making and at the trial itself.[36] To exercise meaningfully the rights accorded to a criminal defendant, one federal court required the defendant to "have some ability to confer intelligently, to testify coherently, and to follow and evaluate the evidence presented."[37] Some state courts applying a Dusky-type standard have gone further, inquiring as to the defendant's decision-making ability at trial. As one court observed, there must be "dialogue and discussion between attorney and client as to tactical decisions concerning the trial."[38] Another required that the defendant be "capable of comprehending counsel and making rational and informed decisions upon counsel's advice. . . ." [39]

In assessing a defendant's ability to interact with counsel, courts distinguish between incapacity and uncooperativeness. For example, in United States v. Turner,[40] the defendant gave "vague, evasive, unresponsive answers, sometimes tantamount to gibberish . . ." [41] in responding to defense counsel's questions. Nevertheless, the district court judge found that the defendant, though suffering from severe anxiety and paranoia, was capable of communicating intelligibly with and assisting counsel but had simply chosen not to do so. The judge, relying on unanimous expert testimony that the defendant was malingering, found him competent.

4. Under federal law, the trial court judge is the decision maker on the issue of the defendant's competence to stand trial.[42] The reports of psychiatrists and other mental health professionals on their evaluation of the defendant's condition and the testimony of those

experts are not binding on the court but are merely one of the facts and circumstances that must be considered by the court in making its determination of the legal question involved.[43] The trial judge must seek not only a clinical judgment but also a judgment that includes the judge's knowledge of criminal trial proceedings.

Nevertheless, the reports and testimony of psychiatrists and other mental health professionals do furnish an evidentiary basis for determining the defendant's competence under the Dusky test.[44] After reviewing the empirical literature on the influence and adequacy of expert testimony on the issue of competency to stand trial, Professors Roesch and Golding concluded:

A. **Psychiatric testimony heavily influences the outcome of judicial decision-making, thus undermining the court's authority.**

B. **Psychiatrists and psychologists typically testify in conclusive terms, often parroting the statutory language, thus depriving the court of the proper evidentiary base for its determination of the defendant's competency. . . .**

C. **Psychiatrists and psychologists often confuse the legal criteria for incompetency with criteria for the existence of mental dysfunction, criminal responsibility, and need for treatment.**

D. **Psychiatrists and psychologists, while competent to judge some aspects of behavioral and psychological processes, are (1) not able to predict future behavior at the level of accuracy often claimed, and (2) not sufficiently conversant with legal matters to be able to judge, within the Dusky criteria, whether or not**

this defendant, facing these charges, in light of the existing evidence, will be able to assist his attorney in a rational manner.[45]

5. In 1981, the American Bar Association (ABA), through its Standing Committee on Association Standards for Criminal Justice, established the Criminal Justice Mental Health Standards Project. The project focused on the interface between mental disability and the criminal process. In part, the project was a response to deficiencies in mental health professional testimony such as those described by Professors Roesch and Golding. The project's standards were approved as American Bar Association policy in 1984 and have been published as Chapter 7 of the American Bar Association Criminal Justice Standards.[46] These standards are available as guidelines for courts and legislatures to consider as they confront issues involving mental disability and the criminal process.

The ABA standards on pretrial evaluations and expert testimony provide a framework for judging the adequacy of forensic evaluations conducted and reports prepared in Stan's case. Standard 7-3.7(a) requires the mental health professional to prepare a complete, written report promptly upon concluding the evaluation. A written report is not required, however, for a defense-initiated evaluation when the defense attorney requests only an oral report.

Standard 7-3.7(b) describes the contents of the evaluator's written report.

The written evaluation report should ordinarily:

(A) **identify the specific matters referred for evaluation;**

(B) **describe the procedures, tests, and techniques used by the evaluator;**

(C) **state the evaluator's clinical findings and opinions on each matter referred for evaluation and indicate specifically those questions, if any, that could not be answered;**

(D) **identify the sources of information and present the factual basis for the evaluator's clinical findings and opinions; and,**

(E) **present the reasoning by which the evaluator utilized the information to reach the clinical findings and opinions. The evaluator should express an opinion on a specific legal criterion or standard only if the opinion is within the scope of the evaluator's specialized knowledge.**

The standard requires the evaluator to include in the written report any statements or information that served as necessary factual predicates for the evaluator's clinical findings or opinions. However, the standard provides that a report prepared on the issue of competency to stand trial should not contain information or opinions concerning either the defendant's mental condition at the time of the alleged crime or any statements made by the defendant regarding the alleged crime or any other crime. This exception was placed in the standards in order to prevent competency evaluations from being misused by prosecutors as a source of investigatory leads into other criminal activity or information bearing on the defendant's mental condition at the time of an alleged crime.

When a defendant's competence to stand trial is being evaluated, Standard 7-4.5(a) informs the evaluator not to consider potential treatment for the defendant unless it is determined that the defendant is incompetent to stand trial. The standard was designed to forestall confusion by mental health professionals and judges between treatment that is necessary to restore the defendant's present mental competency and additional treatment for the defendant's underlying mental illness.

With this brief review of the competency to stand trial issue and the role of the mental health professional in determining competency in the individual case, we turn to the psychiatric reports on the competency issue that were prepared during the twenty-three-month period following Stan's arrest for threatening the president's life. For insights into Stan's relationships with his attorneys, we also discuss letters written by Stan and excerpts from court documents that bear on Stan's mental condition during that time frame.

On December 23, 1983, only one week after Stan was arrested and charged with threatening the president's life, the Assistant United States Attorney serving as prosecutor filed a motion for a hearing to determine Stan's mental competency to stand trial. Four days later, the magistrate found that the government satisfied its burden of establishing reasonable cause for the examination and granted the government's motion.

Chapter I

INSANITY AND CRIMINAL JUSTICE:
Historical Perspective

A. Why Absolve the "Lunatics?"

The mentally ill and feeble minded have for a long time been treated differently in the law.[47] This legal distinction can be traced as far back as the Roman Empire Law.[48] This exception from criminal responsibility survived through the ages to the present day. This section of this review will attempt to articulate a variety of policy and ethical reasons as to why the mentally ill have enjoyed and continue to enjoy an exemption from criminal responsibility.

Any reason to exclude a group of people from punishment for certain acts must rest in the reasons and theory underlying punishment itself.[49] Thus, when one looks at various reasons for punishment advanced throughout the ages, one will have a better understanding of why the mentally ill were often not subject to the full range thereof.

Several classic theories for punishment have been advanced throughout the years. None of these theories however can be applied to the insane. As no theory of punishment fits them, it must follow that punishment is not to apply to the mad.

One theory for why society punishes wayward individuals is to prevent these same individuals from inflicting further harm upon the society.[50] This is best understood as specific deterrence. In essence this theory is very Pavlovian[51] in its nature. By subjecting a violator to negative experiences, the society hopes to elicit an understanding that further rule-breaking will lead to more negative experiences, while following the rules will result in positive experiences.[52] However, this mechanism cannot succeed merely on the "stimulus-response" axis. Some understanding of events surrounding the punishment and of the punishment itself must occur in order for this theory to be effective.[53]

Another theory of punishment is rehabilitation of the wayward members of society.[54] The offenders are incarcerated not just to make them safe,[55] but also more productive members of society.[56] Of course, penance requires that one understands that his actions are wrong, and more importantly, that he has the ability to act "right."[57]

Oftentimes, the desire to educate society on the principles of right and wrong drives the criminal justice system.[58] Two theories are at work. One is that the very process of apprehending, prosecuting and punishing the culprit serves to educate the rest of society as to the prohibited type of conduct, especially as the laws and regulations proliferate at such rate that few individuals can keep pace.[59] The other is that punishment (by being an unpleasant experience) deters other members of society from engaging in unpalatable conduct.[60] By punishing individuals, society affirmatively tells everyone that certain behavior is wrong, and showcases what awaits those who do not heed societal prohibitions.[61]

The oldest theory of punishment is the one of "just deserts." [62] It is aimed directly at the culprit and is based on the idea that the suffering inherent in any punishment is deserved.[63] Through punishment, society exacts its vengeance on those who choose to disregard its rules.[64] The pain that the punishment inflicts on the criminal is in return for the pain that the criminal inflicts on society through his own freely chosen wrongful actions.[65]

Finally, punishment is also inflicted to incapacitate the offender, i.e., to place him in such a surrounding where he can commit no more crimes.[66] (This of course discounts the possibility of crime "on the inside," but even with this factor accounted for, it is undeniable that a person against whom strict control is exercised is not able to cause as much damage as he would otherwise be able to do.)[67] Prison incapacitates dangerous criminals and the society therefore justifiably feels safer.[68]

The mentally ill are not subject to the punishments meted out by the criminal justice system for a variety of reasons. Some, such as "specific deterrence" [69] and "rehabilitation," [70] have to do with the fact that the mentally ill cannot understand the nature of punishment anymore than they can understand the nature of the crime,[71] and the significance of punishment is therefore lost on them.[72] Some, such as "education" [73] or "deterrence" [74] theories have to do with the benefits that inure to the public from such exculpation; because by exculpating the mentally ill, the "right" and "wrong" are brought into focus more clearly.[75] Yet other rationales come from policy reasons that caution against equating a lunatic with a sinister criminal, accordingly making "retribution" inappropriate.[76] Although restraint may seem applicable to both sane and insane, [77] the incapacitation of the insane cannot be viewed as punishment, for they are not merely incapacitated, but treated.[78] Underlying it all, however, is a moral judgment that the mentally ill are not sufficiently "bad" to warrant the condemnation inherent in conviction and criminal sanction.[79] Since "insanity" (and thus lack of responsibility) is a moral view on the part of society, the actions of those involved in the process of separating out the "bad" from the "insane" should conform to that underlying judgment.

B. Science and the Law

Psychiatry was involved in criminal justice at least as far back as the Middle Ages.[80] The two professions that dealt with mental illness at that time (i.e., clergy and physicians) came into contact with the criminal justice system because the law of the times allowed both "idiots" [81] and "lunatics" [82] to be exempted from punishment.[83] Thus a differentiation between those who were sufficiently ill to qualify and those who were not was necessary.[84] The definition of an "idiot" was [A] person who cannot account or number twenty pence, nor can tell who was his father or mother, nor how old he is, etc., so as it may appear he hath no understanding of reason what shall be for his   profit, or what for his loss. But if he have such understanding that he know and understand his letters, and do read by teaching of another man, then it seems he is not a sot or natural fool.[85]

Lunatics on the other hand were defined as persons who suffered from an imbalance of humors.[86] Idiots were completely free from criminal responsibility throughout their lives as they were seen as ever unable to reason and thus form intent.[87] Lunatics on the other hand were free from the responsibility only during the period of raving lunacy, and had to carry all the legal burdens during the periods of clarity.[88] An assessment thus needed to be made whether the person was currently suffering from a disorder or was in his lucid interval.[89] Medical professionals were used to evaluate those whose sanity or other mental faculties were in question,[90] yet the credence they were given did not arise out of the respect for their training or degrees, but rather because the juries believed that they were in a position to closely observe the defendant and thus best able to describe his condition.[91] Thus, although medical opinion could be offered, it rarely was, and when it was, although considered useful, it was not given greater weight than layperson's testimony. This changed greatly with the arrival of the 19th century. Perhaps the most well documented case (prior to modern times) of expert medical testimony in support of mental illness occurred in 1800[92] at the trial of James Hadfield.[93] Mr. Hadfield was accused of attempting to assassinate the King of England,[94] a charge of high treason, punishable by death.[95] Hadfield previously served as a dragoon in an Anglo-French war,[96] where he sustained severe injuries to the head,[97] to the point that the membrane of his brain was visible.[98] His most able counselor, Hon. Thomas Erskine, [99] made the most of the insanity defense.[100] In addition to several lay witnesses who testified as to Hadfield's erratic behavior, [101] Erskine called three different physicians to the stand. [102] Mr. Henry Cline, an eminent surgeon, testified that wounds sustained to the head during the war were sufficient to cause brain damage.[103] Next, Doctor Creighton testified that the Hadfield suffered from delusions;[104] that "he was ordained to die as Jesus Christ." [105] Finally, Mr. Lidderdale,[106] another surgeon, testified that the insanity served as a cause of the discharge from the army.[107]

At the time of James Hadfield's trial though, juries were thought to put little stock in the medical testimony[108] and instead relied on the testimony of lay people, such as friends or acquaintances, [109] The trial helped to start a process of changing these attitudes. The testimony of a psychiatrist is now considered to be most useful,[110] although general physicians (especially if they have been treating the defendant for some period of time) also offer testimony.[111] It has been noted that juries tend to believe "independent" (i.e., court-appointed) experts more than an expert for any particular side.[112]

Although medical professionals are generally held in higher esteem then before,[113] some juries have disregarded medical testimony to find defendants sane on the basis of lay testimony when such testimony contradicted that of a psychiatrist.[114] Courts have upheld such verdicts. [115] It is the contention of this study that the juries disregard professional testimony[116] because such testimony has fallen into disrepute due to the very nature of "battling experts." [117] When psychiatrists are allowed to testify on issues beyond their competence (e.g., morals, dangerousness) their testimony ceases to be legitimate expert testimony. The contention is that if psychiatry is to keep its legitimate place within the criminal justice system, it must be nothing more than an objective evaluator of medical information, and leave the determination of moral culpability to non-physicians. Both policy and medical ethics call for such a result.

C. Various Judicial Tests for Insanity.

Mental illness, however defined, has for a very long time been viewed as an exculpatory answer to a charge of crime.[118] Almost eight hundred years ago Lord Bracton announced the principle that people who do not know what they are doing, cannot be held responsible for their actions.[119] The premise of the "ability to discern between good and evil" [120] test for criminal responsibility rested on a notion that children under the age of seven, (i.e., under the "age of reason") cannot be held responsible for their actions. [121] So too, the courts of the time reasoned, if a man is like a child who cannot tell a difference, he too cannot be held responsible for his actions.[122] The test for what constitutes sufficient affliction to be held not criminally responsible has changed, but the basic proposition that at least some of the mentally ill should not be dealt with within the bounds of the criminal justice system has remained largely unchanged.[123]

Since Lord Bracton's original pronouncement on what will suffice to have a person adjudged not responsible for his action, the common law tried several different approaches to identify those that are sufficiently ill to escape criminal punishment.[124] For example, in Rex v. Arnold,[125] Justice Tracy instructed the jury to acquit the defendant if they found that he was "a man that is totally deprived of his understanding and memory, and doth not know what he is doing, no more than an infant, or a wild beast, or a brute, [for] such a one is never the object of punishment." [126] One can conclude from such a definition that the underlying idea under the Not Guilty by Reason of Insanity acquittal was total deprivation of senses.[127] While medical professionals could be used in such a circumstance, such complete "lunacy" should have been evident even without medical testimony. As described above, this "complete madness"[128] notion was successfully challenged by Thomas Erskine in the trial of James Hadfield, [129] and so the involvement of medical professionals became more pronounced.[130]

A new test was announced after deliberation in the House of Lords, subsequent to an acquittal of Daniel M'Naghten of the charge of treason.[131] The M'Naghten test also specifically made "disease or defect of mind" a prerequisite to an insanity acquittal, rather than just a general "wild beast" state.[132] Additionally, their lordships stated that in order to be acquitted, one "labouring under such a defect of reason, from disease of the mind, [did] not ... know the nature and quality of the act he was doing; or, if he did know it, that he did not know what he was doing was wrong." [133] Thus, mental illness was necessary, but insufficient for the acquittal. In so deciding a case, the House of Lords virtually assured that science and medicine would stay involved with the law.

The M'Naghten test survived for a very long time[134] and in many jurisdictions is still in use today.[135] The major (albeit brief) departure and expansion of the availability of the insanity defense came in 1954, when the D.C. Circuit handed down its decision in Durham v. United States.[136] The Durham court held it to be irrelevant whether defendant knew right from wrong,[137] and instead relied on a "product test." [138] The court stated that the accused is not to be held criminally liable if his criminal act was a "product of mental disease or defect." [139] Durham was the high point of involving science in the criminal adjudication, in the sense that it called for the jury to hear all pertinent medical testimony on mental disease.[140] However, the court did not subscribe to the notion that the presence of mental disease or psychiatric testimony would serve as a final determination of sanity.[141] Indeed, one of the reasons the D.C. Circuit adopted the new rule was to separate scientific determinations from the legal ones.[142] The court stated that the "[j]uries will continue to make moral judgments, still operating under the fundamental precept that 'Our collective conscience does not allow punishment where it cannot impose blame,'" [143] while not focusing exclusively on "whether he displayed particular symptoms which medical science has long recognized do not necessarily, or even typically, accompany even the most serious mental disorder."[144]

Durham was abandoned in 1972.[145] Today many states continue to follow the M'Naghten test or the American Legal Institute (ALI) test.[146] (There was a trend away from the ALI test back to M'Naghten following the NGRI acquittal of John Hinckley.)[147] The ALI test is centered on whether or not the defendant lacked "substantial capacity" to "appreciate the criminality [wrongfulness] of his conduct or to conform his conduct to the requirements of the law." [148] The ALI test, although at first glance is quite similar to the M'Naghten rule, answers one of the main criticisms of M'Naghten,[149] insofar as it does not rely as heavily on actually "knowing right from wrong," [150] instead focusing on the "capacity" [151] to make that distinction. The main criticism of this test has been that the words "substantial capacity" are not defined, thus potentially causing confusion in the experts and the juries.[152] Differences among experts that result from the lack of precision of the ALI rule are likely to lead to the "battle" of these experts, perhaps confusing the jury even further.[153]

Throughout time, many different definitions of criminal insanity have been tried, [154] yet a perfect one has yet to be found. Some, like the ALI test, are deemed to be too imprecise,[155] some like M'Naghten, too rigid.[156] Yet, irrespective of what test a modern jurisdiction uses, they rely on the help of psychiatrists in verifying that for the criminal justice purposes, the person in question is insane.[157] To what degree such help should be used is the focus of this review.

Chapter II

PRESENT STATUS IN U.S.

A. Psychiatric Involvement Today

The role of psychiatrist in today's criminal justice system is varied and multidimensional.[158] Psychiatrists can get involved in any stage of the process, from the initial hearing determining competency to stand trial,[159] to testifying at trial as to the mental state of the accused,[160] to post-sentencing[161] (or post-acquittal)[162] treatment. The testimony of the psychiatrist can be based not only upon personal evaluation of the defendant,[163] but also on such questionable techniques as evaluation of the other testimony in the case[164] or even a hypothetical question propounded by counsel.[165] Needless to say, the testimony offered at these proceedings may not always be grounded in hard science.[166] Additionally, at several stages of the process, the defendant may be entitled to his own (as opposed to the one working for the state) psychiatric expert witness.[167] As can be expected, when one psychiatrist works for one side and another for a different side, the conclusions as to culpability do not always coincide.[168] A "battle of the experts" often ensues where the medical profession is at its worst, and the jury oftentimes disregards the testimony of both physicians in favor of the far less scientific lay testimony.[169] While many argue that the "battle of the experts" is the disease afflicting the criminal justice system,[170] this study argues that it is but a symptom of a larger problem, namely excessive entanglement between medicine and criminal law.

Currently, psychiatric testimony is often unmoored from the hard psychiatric science, and ventures into the realm of law and morality. This has caused some to argue in favor of abandoning the introduction of psychiatric testimony altogether.[171] On the other hand, psychiatric testimony is deemed to be quite useful in shedding light on the mental processes of the accused, causing some to argue for psychiatrists to be allowed to give their opinions on whether the accused could not "help himself" in committing a crime.[172] Neither of these two extremes is appropriate. Psychiatric testimony is indeed quite useful if one uses it to elucidate defendant's mental health. However, such testimony is irrelevant if one is trying to affix responsibility. It then follows that the testimony should be geared towards answering the first question. In order to answer the question of defendant's mental health, a psychiatrist needs to confine himself to issues of medical fact. The testimony should resemble a conversation between two psychiatrists upon a transfer of the patient. Thus issues like diagnosis, treatment, signs and symptoms would be covered (as well as reasoning for coming to a given conclusion) while issues of responsibility, morality and future dangerousness will be left for others to testify to and decide. Testimony thus limited would revolve around medical issues, i.e., those on which physicians have a specialized knowledge. Not only would such testimony be more scientifically sound,[173] but also more ethically appropriate, as discussed in Part V. This approach would allow the jury to hear testimony on issues that they may not be familiar with (i.e., different psychiatric syndromes, manifestations of disease, etc) from an expert, while precluding the expert from using his position to foist upon the jury his own moral judgments, an issue on which he is no more an expert than a given juror.

The current level of actual psychiatric entanglement with the law is revealed below.

1. Competency to Stand Trial

At the earliest stage of the criminal proceedings, a psychiatrist can be used to evaluate the patient to see if he is "competent" to stand trial.[174] Competency is not a medical term, but a legal one.[175] A defendant is adjudged competent if "he has sufficient present ability to consult with his lawyer with a reasonable degree of rational understanding--and whether he has a rational as well as factual understanding of the proceedings against him." [176] A finding of incompetence halts all further proceedings indefinitely, until such time as competence can be regained.[177] Up until relatively recently, a person found to be incompetent to stand trial would be subject to a lifetime of commitment in a psychiatric institution in lieu of punishment.[178] This practice was disapproved by the Supreme Court in Jackson v. Indiana.[179] Today, a person found to be incompetent should be subject to hospitalization only for a period of time necessary to determine the likelihood of regaining competency.[180] Indeed, hospitalization is not even required.[181] The observation and evaluation of an incompetent person can be done on an outpatient basis.[182] If at any point the psychiatrist believes that the defendant is able to meet the competency standard,[183] he must file a report with a court that will adjudicate competence.[184] In practice, such psychiatric determinations are almost always deferred to.[185]

The evaluation is generally performed by a psychiatrist specifically designated by the court[186] and is done in the psychiatrist's office, court clinic, or jail.[187] Often the examination occurs at a mental institution.[188] In either case, the examination is done by a professional in government's employ.[189] The examining psychiatrist prepares a report of the examination for the court with copies for the prosecuting and defense counsel.[190] A defendant may employ his own psychiatrist,[191] but if a "battle of the experts" ensues as a result of divergent findings between the court-appointed "independent" expert, and the defendant-retained expert, the former is likely to be given more credence by the court[192] Because of the awesome power that the court-appointed psychiatrist may have on the outcome of the case,[193] the competing sides may use the psychiatric examination and testimony to their own maximum advantage regardless of the actual scientific underpinnings of such procedures.[194] Some believe that even the court itself, presumably the most impartial player in the system, may utilize the process to avoid for example granting bail.[195] Furthermore, there have been accusations that courts use the competency evaluations to justify what it wants to do with the defendant,[196] and a psychiatrist may find himself used as a cover by the court or prosecuting attorney. [197]

As competency is a legal standard and not a medical one,[198] psychiatrists are torn between the desires to have their work correspond to the acceptable scientific standards on the one hand,[199] and on the other hand to have the report fit within the legal framework of "incompetence." [200] A professional so "divided against himself" cannot for long maintain the high code of medical ethics and is prone to slip to a position where he becomes more than an impartial scientist or a healer, but an advocate for one side in a legal argument.

2. Testimony at Trial

The second point at which psychiatrists get involved with the criminal justice system is at trial, [201] testifying for either the defense or the prosecution as to the defendant's culpability in his criminal act.[202] The psychiatric testimony as to culpability centers on the insanity rules outlined in Part II, supra. At trial, psychiatric testimony oftentimes becomes a "battle of the experts," [203] (usually more so than at the "incompetence" stage) [204] where the court and jury are trying to elucidate the psychiatrist's professional medical opinion on essentially a legal issue.[205] Psychiatrists are expected to testify not only to the mental state of an individual, i.e., whether or not an individual suffers from mental disease (a relatively objective medical diagnosis), but also on whether or not the defendant is insane (a strictly legal term, bounded by the insanity defense rules).[206]

Traditionally, neither physicians nor lay witnesses were allowed to testify on the "ultimate question," i.e., whether the defendant is "responsible." [207] This prohibition has survived to the present day,[208] although, perhaps in name and form only, rather than substance.[209] The reason for refusing to entertain psychiatrists' testimony on the issue of responsibility stems from

the idea that responsibility is a legal finding that the
jury cannot cede to any individual or even a panel of
experts,[210] Traditionally, psychiatrists were also not
allowed to testify as to "test questions," [211] i.e., whether
the defendant satisfied the requisite test for insanity (e.g.,
whether the defendant knew right from wrong),[212] Thus,
psychiatric testimony was limited essentially to medical
issues.[213] Again, the reason that was advanced for
keeping psychiatrists from testifying about appreciation
of "right and wrong" (or any other legal standard for
that matter) is that the jury and not a witness (expert or
otherwise) should be the ultimate judge on this issue.[214]

Notwithstanding the above objections, recently, the
courts have been more and more tolerant of psychiatrists
being asked and answering "test questions." [215] Indeed,
allowing testimony on "test questions" is the rule in the
majority of jurisdictions.[216] The Model Penal Code allows
an expert (presumably a mental health professional) to
testify as to the capacity of the defendant to appreciate
the nature and/or criminality of his conduct. [217] The
proponents of this new rule respond to the objections
of the years past by suggesting that the jury would be
better served and better informed by "expert" testimony.
[218] This view, however, fails to take into account the
reality that when psychiatrists are asked to testify on
"test questions," the defense and prosecution "experts"
will almost invariably come to different conclusions.[219]
When such divergent views are presented to the jury,
the jury "tend[s] to supplant the factual detail upon which
the decision for responsibility should ideally be based.
... The jury is left with the impression that it must choose
between the experts ..." [220]

The jury, if convinced that the defendant is sane, will presumably rely (at least to some extent) on the testimony of the psychiatrist for the state. [221] Thus, this testimony would be one of the reasons of someone being sent to jail. On the other hand, the jury, if convinced the defendant is insane, will presumably base its findings (at least in part) on the testimony of a defense psychiatrist. In this case, the psychiatrist's testimony will be responsible for potentially letting a criminal, or at the very least, a dangerous human being, roam free in an unprotected society.[222] In both cases, psychiatrists face an ethical dilemma as to the appropriate course of action, and this article proposes a solution to this ethical quandary. Additionally, of course, the standards for "insanity" are different between the different courts,[223] and thus psychiatrists are almost forced to come to different conclusions on sanity in different jurisdictions, even though these conclusions are based on the same clinical data. In a scientific world to which psychiatrists belong by virtue of their belonging to the medical profession, identical data should lead to identical results.[224] When the identical data leads to divergent results, the conclusion is inescapable that something other than a scientific approach to the clinical problem at hand has taken place. If that is indeed true, then the psychiatrists involved are not living up to the standards of their profession.

3. Competency at Execution

Even if an accused is found competent to stand trial, and then found guilty (i.e., either does not raise or is not successful in his insanity defense) and is sentenced to death, he cannot be executed if he ceases being competent at any time between the verdict and the carrying out of the sentence.[225] It is, then, of no surprise that the question of competence arises quite often in the context of execution.[226] Psychiatrists are again called on to examine the prisoner and to render their expert opinion on the matter.[227]

The involvement of psychiatrists in competency for execution adjudication is nothing new, but until the 1980s, the involvement was rather low profile.[228] One of the reasons was that in years gone by executions occurred quite soon after trial, so there was little need for an evaluation separate from that conducted prior to trial.[229] Additionally, any deterioration that used to occur prior to the advent of psychotropic medication was the result of progressing disease.[230] Typically, un-medicated disease was slow to progress,[231] and thus a person who was competent to stand trial would likely remain competent at the time of the execution.[232] By contrast, after the advent of antipsychotic medication, post-trial deterioration could well be the result of withdrawing medication.[233] The deterioration in such circumstances was much more rapid;[234] the prisoner who was quite competent to stand trial could rapidly become incompetent thereafter if the medications were withdrawn.[235] Because of the above possibility, the State had to institute a separate procedure to evaluate competence prior to execution.[236]

The procedures established in response to the need for separate competency evaluation prior to execution were originally quite informal.[237] Not until Ford v. Wainwright[238] was decided in 1986, establishing a constitutional prohibition on executing the insane, was there a requirement for any adjudicatory proceedings in the matter.[239] Indeed as late as the 1950s, the

Court viewed execution reprieves as no different from other clemency issues, best left to the discretion of the executive.[240] The executive could base his decision on psychiatric reports, but was not required to do so.[241] Psychiatrists were then just advisors to the executive authority.[242] Additionally, psychiatrists could simply subvert the justice system by refusing to notify prison authorities of any improvement in mental health of the prisoners in their care.[243] Once a warden ordered a transfer of a prisoner to a psychiatric unit, the psychiatrist in charge could simply keep him there indefinitely, thus essentially "lifting" the death sentence.[244]

After Ford, the procedure for evaluating pre-execution competence has become more formalized and vested in the judicial as opposed to the executive branch.[245] The procedure today is very similar to a trial.[246] That decision requires that a hearing be held in order to determine competency for execution; and that such hearing is to be a de novo review of the incompetence claim.[247] As it is now an evidentiary hearing, by its very nature it requires evidence to be adduced. Thus, psychiatrists are given yet another opportunity to participate in a legal process, with all trap doors attendant thereto.

4. Medicating the Prisoners

Psychiatrists can also be involved in the criminal justice system outside of the courthouse (albeit still within the criminal justice system). The criminal justice system uses psychiatrists in order to provide medical regimens to inmates.[248] The most common use is for psychiatrists to medicate those individuals who suffer from some sort of mental disease, but are confined in mental institutions. However, psychiatrists are also used to administer medications to incompetent individuals, in hopes of making them competent to stand trial,[249] as well as occasionally, to make them competent enough to be executed.[250] In two recent decisions, the criminal justice system has deemed the use of psychiatrists to involuntarily administer medications to be acceptable and indeed desirable,[251] a proposition that at least at first glance does not correspond to the "primum non nocere" norm of medical ethics. [252]

The most authoritative, albeit incomplete, pronouncement on the issue of pre-trial forced medication came in 1992. In Riggins v. Nevada,[253] the defendant (petitioner) was medicated against his will, was convicted, sentenced to die, and then challenged his conviction and sentence on the grounds that forcible medication was used.[254] The Court refused to allow such medication when the state could not show that medication was needed to maintain competence,[255] and/or that less drastic alternatives were unavailable.[256] The Court noted that pre-trial medication is impermissible "absent a finding of overriding justification and ... medical appropriateness." [257] (It is noteworthy that the Court did not say medical necessity).[258] As there was no showing in Riggins that the trial could not proceed absent medication, [259] the first prong was not satisfied.

It is far from clear what the Court meant when it said "medically appropriate." The minimalist approach to this statement would simply evaluate the efficacy of treatment offered. Thus, if a given medication restores competence it is medically appropriate. This however, does not take into account the patient's own wishes. In a broader sense, no treatment unless consented to is appropriate for a given patient, no matter how efficacious it may be. To say otherwise would be to start on a slippery slope towards such "treatments" as forced sterilization. They are most certainly "medically appropriate" in a sense that they are highly efficacious in achieving their goal of limiting certain individual's reproductive ability. Nevertheless, one is hard-pressed to state that these "treatments" are indeed "appropriate." Thus, unless there is an emergent circumstance, where lives are threatened or where patient's consent cannot be obtained, an un-consented treatment should not be considered "medically appropriate."

The issue of whether it is legal to medicate someone for the sole purpose of restoring competence to stand trial is currently before the Supreme Court.[260] The Eight Circuit Court of Appeals has held that such use of medical knowledge is appropriate.[261] In Sell v. United States,[262] a split panel of the Eighth Circuit held that the government's interest in bringing an incompetent defendant to trial is a sufficient reason to have him medicated against his will.[263] (As the defendant was incompetent,[264] and as competency could be, at least potentially, restored via medication, [265] the "medical appropriateness" prong was satisfied, at least insofar as the treatment was efficacious).[266] In that case the court acknowledged that there was no reason, such as danger to self or others, except the desire to bring the prisoner to trial, that would necessitate medication.[267] The court's reasoning allows psychiatrists to be employed for purposes that although medically appropriate,[268] would go against the interest of the patient insofar as retention of autonomy over medical decisions is a primary interest.

Shortly following the Sell decision, the Eighth Circuit also dealt with the issue of whether it is permissible to medicate someone against his will solely for the purpose of having an individual regain competence for execution.[269] In Singleton v. Norris,[270] a 6-5 majority (hearing the case en banc) held that indeed this too is permissible.[271] If Sell could be defended on the grounds that at the very least the defendant once restored to competency will be able to live a "normal" life (albeit behind bars), Singleton suggests that psychiatric knowledge can be used for the purposes of ending life.[272] This is inimical to all the training and education that physicians get, and is no different than a physician directly administering lethal drugs in an execution setting.[273]

5. Treating the Acquitted

Perhaps the most "medical" [274] of all points of psychiatric involvement in the criminal justice system is the treatment of NGRI acquitted. Some jurisdictions exercise mandatory commitment following an NGRI acquittal,[275] and some permissive.[276] The goals served by commitment are two-fold. One, as mentioned in Part II, supra, is restraint of those individuals who commit crimes as a result of their illness.[277] The other is to treat and rehabilitate (in the medical sense of the word) these mentally ill individuals. These two goals do not always coincide; consequently psychiatrists at least occasionally end up treating people in a manner that is suboptimal for the clinical presentation.[278] In these instances it is rather clear that psychiatrists are not practicing good medicine, instead they are serving as mere extensions of the penal system.

B. The Consequences of Being Adjudged Insane

Irrespective of what test the courts have used, the tradition that those suffering from "insanity" should not be held criminally responsible is a deeply rooted one.[279] If the defendant satisfied the test du jour, he would not be liable to criminal sanctions.[280] The rationale for such treatment of the insane is manifold and has changed with the times. As noted above, for many years it was thought to be improper to punish a child who couldn't reason (at least according to the Bible).[281] Consequently, it was just as improper to punish someone who was nothing more than a child.[282] Throughout the years, another notion, that it is rather pointless to administer punishment to someone who will learn nothing from such punishment and will not be deterred from further criminal activity as a result of his insanity, has taken hold.[283]

Originally (i.e., in the medieval times), those found to be of "unsound mind" at the time of the commission of the crime were not held criminally liable, and could be free to conduct their lives as any other person would have,[284] except that at least until the seventeenth century the property of the defendant so acquitted was still subject to forfeiture.[285] The check on such release of dangerous elements into society was the fact that under early tests for "madness" very few dangerous individuals were acquitted.[286] The degree of "madness" to be demonstrated had to be truly extreme in order to be exculpated, and few defendants satisfied the test.[287]

However, those that did satisfy the test were indeed released.

Although the defendants were not held criminally liable, they were not "acquitted" in the full sense of the word.[288] Instead, the jury rendered a verdict of guilty, together with the special verdict of "lunacy," and the combination of these two verdicts invariably led to a Royal Pardon.[289] The prisoner was then released with no other special provisions for his care.[290] In 1800, however, the Criminal Lunatics Act required those defendants found "mad" to be committed to a secure institution "until His Majesty's pleasure be known." [291] This was the beginning of institutionalizing the criminally insane. It is worth noting that the institutionalization was for an indefinite[292] (and potentially life-long) period even in cases where the incarceration in prison would have been of a relatively short duration.[293] Indeed, the defendant in one of the most celebrated cases of that time (the very case that prompted the passage of the Criminal Lunatics Act), James Hadfield, was acquitted of trying to assassinate the King,[294] but was nonetheless committed to Bethlem Hospital.[295] That the purpose of such confinement was not to treat but to preventively detain,[296] can be evidenced from the very language of the statute. The Act notably did not call for detainment until "return to sanity," but rather until the King chose to release the prisoner.

Indeed, it has been said that in the Victorian England "most criminal lunatics remained in goal."[297] But even when lunatics were separated from the general prison population and institutionalized in separate institutions, the confinement in these secure institutions often did not differ much from prison.[298]

Similar treatment was accorded to lunatics in other countries as well. For instance, in China, where "madness" was never an exculpation, but grounds for sentence mitigation,[299] starting in the 17th century, those deemed to be "mad" were released into the custody of their family.[300] The people so released had to be kept manacled, [301] and the family, under the threat of a rather severe punishment, had to control the individual.[302] However, this "humane" treatment of the insane soon gave way to forced registration and institutionalization.[303] As in England, in China the original intent of the confinement was not to treat, but to isolate dangerous individuals from the society.[304]

The requirement of post-NGRI acquittal confinement largely persists to this day.[305] Although the stated goal of confinement today is medical cure,[306] as opposed to the former goal of isolation, confinement and psychiatrists are too often used for purposes other than treatment.[307] Too often, irrespective of the committed person's actual state of mind, the commitment is continued.[308] Furthermore, the psychiatric profession at times advocated continued commitment of those individuals who have retained their "sanity" but continue to manifest "personality disorders." [309] This type of treatment suggests that the true goal behind institutionalization is punitive rather than rehabilitative in nature. The courts have not been shy in ignoring psychiatric recommendations for release in those who reacquired their sanity. For example, in Francois v. Henderson,[310] the judge refused to release a patient who for over five years exhibited no symptoms of mental disease or other abnormalities on the ground that such behavior is indeed evidence of mental illness, as the prisoner is faking sanity! [311]

While it can be argued that the mentally ill ought to be punished, it is the contention of this study that even so, it is still wholly improper to use medical professionals to mete out the punishment. The above statement applies with equal force irrespective of whether the patient is confined in a mental institution or has his liberty otherwise restricted (e.g., by having to participate in an outpatient program) if such restriction serves no legitimate medical end.

As can be seen from some of the above examples, psychiatric involvement have not eliminated arbitrariness or brought about an exclusively scientific approach to the mental health problems encountered in the criminal justice system. Instead, medical pronouncements are used to cloak judicial preferences with a mantle of scientific legitimacy. A physician thus used becomes an instrument of the penal system as opposed to a healer or even a scientist in search of truth. Such a system cannot be deemed to be satisfactory.

Chapter III

PRESENT STATUS IN U.K.

Some have argued that the underlying problem with the American conception of the psychiatry-criminal justice interaction is that it relies on independent witnesses for the defense and prosecution. [312] It is argued that by being a witness for either side the psychiatrist has a stake in the outcome, and that in and of itself is unprofessional.[313] The proposed solution is replacing "hired guns" with an independent panel, composed of a number of psychiatrists whose conclusions are to be accepted by the court.[314] The argument goes as follows: Because the psychiatrists are independent they would not have a stake in the outcome, and because there would be no "hired guns," there would be no "expert battles," an affair that diminishes the medical profession as a whole.[315] For the reasons set forth below, it is the contention of this author that this solution would not solve the fundamental problem of medical professionals operating outside of their area of expertise, and beyond what can be considered ethical medical behavior.

As can be imagined, the American system of psychiatric involvement in the adjudicatory process is not the only option available, and has not been universally embraced. The former Soviet Union[316] the People's Republic of China, [317] and USSR's successor, the Russian Federation[318] are but a few states that employ different process and procedures to separate the competent from the incompetent and the sane from the insane. This section will describe the operation of the system and highlight a specific case to show that merely switching from partisan experts to independent panels is unlikely to resolve the problem of psychiatrists straying beyond medical issues and on to the field of moral judgments about the accused.

A. Psychiatric Evaluation in the Soviet Criminal Justice System

In the USSR, the court or the Procuracy[319] could order a psychiatric examination of the accused. The examination was conducted by a team of psychiatrists[320] appointed by the court (or Procuracy). The team consisted of three experts who conducted their evaluation based on the guidelines published by Serbsky Institute of Forensic Psychiatry.[321] Following such guidelines was mandatory.[322] The patient-accused was not entitled to challenge the proceedings in any way, either in person, through counsel, or through family.[323]   The team of psychiatrists was asked to address several questions. First, does the accused suffer from any mental illness? Second, is his illness such that he did not "realize the significance of his actions" or that he "could not control them?" Finally, and most troubling, the psychiatrists were asked whether the accused was "socially dangerous." The reason the second and third questions are troubling is because both of them ask a psychiatrist to pass on a legal proposition. Medical knowledge is either irrelevant or of very little use in answering these questions. The answer to these questions is likely to be based on the psychiatrist's worldview (e.g., what constitutes danger to his society)[324] as opposed to any scientific fact or criterion.

The findings of the forensic psychiatrists were submitted to the court[325] that held a summary, often ex parte hearing where it determined whether to accept the findings and recommendations.[326] In practice the reports were never challenged,[327] and the determinations of the psychiatrists were accepted.[328]

In this system, the psychiatrists are again employed in a way that requires them to make pronouncements on the issue of legal responsibility.[329] Granted, no "battle of the experts" ensues,[330] as the only report of any significance is that submitted by the "independent" medical experts,[331] but nonetheless, the medical profession takes upon itself tasks that it is not designed to handle, while the legal profession cedes its authority and expertise to professionals from another field.

The abuse of psychiatry in the Soviet Union has been well-documented [332] and this article will not dwell on its nature. There are now an increasing number of reports that similar misuse of psychiatry occurs in the People's Republic of China,[333] among other countries. It is hardly surprising that a repressive regime would attempt to use medicine for its own means.[334] However, with a process outlined above in place, a country need not be repressive for the science of psychiatry to be put to use in an area beyond its scope of expertise, thus perverting the science by asking it to make scientifically unsupported judgments.[335] With this system of psychiatric participation, psychiatrists invariably will and do attach their own values to the evaluation of the accused.[336] An "independent" psychiatrist is essentially given a free hand to project his personal and societal sympathies and antipathies onto a patient and to have his "scientific" conclusion mirror his moral world outlook.[337] Of course in a repressive regime, a psychiatrist whose moral outlook mirrors that of a political accused is unlikely to find himself as one of the examining experts.[338] Nevertheless, the underlying problem remains the same irrespective of what views psychiatrists actually hold.

The fact that a system need not be repressive or have procedures shrouded in secrecy (as they were in Soviet times) in order to enmesh the medical profession and its "independent experts" in a legal and political quagmire, is best illustrated by the recent and ongoing case of Russian Colonel Yuri Budanov.

B. The Case of Colonel Yuri Budanov

Colonel Budanov was a senior federal (i.e., Russian government) military officer engaged in the military operations in the breakaway republic of Chechnya.[339] In March 2000, while conducting a military operation, Mr. Budanov captured, kidnapped and strangled Elza Kungaeva, an 18-year old Chechen girl.[340] The colonel was indicted on charges of exceeding authority,[341] kidnapping,[342] rape[343] (later dropped),[344] and murder.[345] Originally, the defense claimed that the girl was a sniper,[346] and a part of a terrorist network; consequently, Budanov did not commit murder, but merely exceeded his authority by killing her.[347] However, later, the defense claimed that at any rate, Col. Budanov was "nevmeniaem" [348] at the time of the crime.[349] In the context of the plea it signified a claim that at the time of the crime the colonel was in such a mental state as to prevent him from understanding his actions.

The case was complicated by several political considerations. First, the Russian government vehemently denied any human rights abuses in Chechnya.[350] Second, up until the episode with Ms. Kungaeva, Col. Budanov was a model and decorated officer,[351] and a hero to many; thus any aspersions upon him were often viewed as casting a pall over the entire Russian Army.[352] It is in this situation that the court had to work.

As required by law, Mr. Budanov was sent to undergo a psychiatric evaluation.[353] Local psychiatrists viewed him as completely sane and thus responsible for his actions.[354] A second evaluation was then ordered.[355] The results of this second examination were never officially revealed.[356] A third assessment of the colonel was then conducted,[357] this time at Moscow's prestigious Serbsky Institute for Forensic Psychiatry,[358] home to the most pre-eminent specialists in the field in all of the Russian Federation. The physicians from that evaluation concluded that Budanov was not able to realize the significance of his actions.[359] Thus, the court was faced with two contradictory psychiatric conclusions. Instead of querying the experts or allowing for their direct and cross-examination, the court at the behest of attorneys representing the family of the victim[360] ordered a fourth exam.[361] This exam was again conducted at the Serbsky Institute,[362] and (unsurprisingly) again resulted in the finding of insanity at the time of the offense.[363] Indeed, this fourth opinion stated that all previous studies underestimated the true nature of Budanov's illness.[364] Again the experts were not questioned, and although both the prosecution and the victim's counsel objected to the findings of the experts, the court accepted them without any hesitation, [365] and acquitted Col. Budanov.[366]

It cannot go unsaid that the last evaluation of the colonel occurred at the time when Chechen terrorists seized a Moscow theater along with several hundred hostages.[367]   Although this may be mere coincidence, the possibility that this event that shocked Russia played a role in the psychiatrist's evaluation cannot be discounted. The psychiatrists once again were given the opportunity to project their personal feeling towards the war in Chechnya, towards Chechen resistance fighters (or terrorists, depending on one's point of view), on acceptable methods of combating terrorism, on the Russian Army, and on Chechens in general. Far be it from the author of this review to accuse these psychiatrists of actually succumbing to the opportunity; however, it is the author's view that such opportunity should never be presented, lest the temptation is too great. Regardless of how conscientious and upright an individual is, when asked a question of morals he will almost inevitably incorporate his life's experience, political leanings, and social views into the answer. It is at this point that the physician stops being a healer and ends up being a part of the criminal justice system, and such a transformation is incompatible with medical ethics. Granted, a physician may tailor his medical opinions to fit within a given political situation as well; however, medical opinions that are "tailored" to politics can be easier exposed than moral opinions. As medical opinions are based in science (even if not fully precise science), the falsity of testimony not grounded in science can be rebutted by someone who is an expert in a given field of medicine. A moral opinion cannot be false by definition, and therefore cannot be rebutted.

The Soviet-Russian system of independent psychiatric panels at its core is no more objectionable from the viewpoint of medical ethics or legal policy than the American system of witnesses for either side, so long as it is limited strictly to the diagnosis of the disease. However, once psychiatrists start operating in the land of morals, and in the realm of right and wrong, they are acting contrary to medical ethics regardless of what system they participate in.

*Judiciis est judicare secundum
allegata et probata.*

~

**It is the duty of a judge to make
his decisions based on facts which have been
alleged and proved.**

Chapter IV

PSYCHOLOGICAL PROBLEMS

Psychiatrists serve multiple roles in the criminal justice system. They are treating physicians, scientists who investigate and report, state employees, representatives of the medical profession in general, and citizens possessed of special knowledge that may be useful to the courts of law. With so many hats to wear, psychiatrists potentially have several allegiances. The question then is to whom they owe their loyalty in cases when there is a conflict of loyalties. Some have suggested that because of the numerous incarnations of a forensic physician, a new ethical paradigm be adopted, one that is different from the traditional ethical duties of "primum non nocere."

One alternative advanced is the ethics of "truth." [368] According to Paul Appelbaum, the leading advocate of the "ethics of truth" the doctor is acting ethically so long as he is objectively evaluating a patient, and then testifies as to his findings.[369] Under this theory, it is irrelevant what the outcome of such testimony would be, so long as the testifying physician was striving for scientific truth.[370] The problem with this approach is that it essentially subsumes all of the forensic psychiatrist's roles into one role of a researcher. This approach may very well work for a forensic pathologist, who merely evaluates evidence (be it bullet trajectory, bite marks, or whatever else) and presents his testimony based on evaluation of such rather impersonal evidence. The theory does not work for forensic psychiatry, because evidence is the live person, and evaluation of evidence (at least in order to get a full and complete picture) necessarily involves evaluation of an individual. When such evaluation occurs, the individual being evaluated becomes (however briefly) a patient of the evaluator.[371]   If that is so, the evaluator's duties with respect to that individual must be no different than any other physician's duties to any other patient.

The approach that makes the forensic psychiatrist owe primary allegiance to the patient, does not ignore forensic psychiatrist's other duties, i.e., the one he owes to the state (his employer), the public at large, and the medical profession. Instead, this approach suggests that whenever there is a physician-patient interaction (even if no treatment or further interactions are offered or contemplated) the physician's obligation to a given patient takes primacy.

Accepting the above proposition, this article relies on twin principles of "no harm" [372] and "consent" [373] to build a foundation of ethical behavior by psychiatrists. Additionally, the "professionalism" principle is a "final check" to be employed once the other two are satisfied. Utilizing these principles, the psychiatrist does not compromise his duties to the patient, while the justice system is not robbed of the wisdom and knowledge of science.

A. Basic Principles

The two principles of ethical behavior by psychiatrists are complementary and can hardly work one without one another. Yet for ease of understanding and structure, they will be discussed separately.

1. The "No Harm" Principle

Before a physician embarks on a course of action with a given patient he must pose a question to himself. The question should ask whether the procedure or action sought to be undertaken is medically appropriate.[374] If the proposed procedure is not medically appropriate, then it can be said that no medical benefit is derived from it.[375] If no medical benefit accrues, it can be inferred that medical harm results. It results either from the progress of the disease in the face of wrong treatment or from the side-effects of the treatment itself. In these situations medical harm outweighs medical benefit.

The question then arises, does not the patient experience a benefit from having his wishes followed if he requests a treatment that the physician believes to be futile or otherwise incorrect, and if so, does that benefit not balance the harm? The answer suggested here is "no." A patient's consent is necessary[376] but insufficient for a physician to initiate treatment. The "primum non nocere" principle as envisioned here requires a physician using his specialized knowledge to evaluate scientific risks and benefits and satisfy himself that the risks are medically acceptable. If he cannot so satisfy himself, it should not matter what the patient's desires are. Once the physician does satisfy himself that the risks are medically acceptable, he then proceeds to enquire of the patient whether the patient is willing to undergo these risks.

To borrow on an example used in Part III.A.4, it is not unethical for a physician to participate in a procedure that results in sterilization of someone, because such procedure is efficacious. However, prior to engaging in

such a procedure, he must obtain a patient's consent.[377]
A physician's evaluation of clinical harms and benefits
is therefore a condition precedent for taking any further
actions.

This reasoning applies only to medical (physiologic)
issues, because it is on these issues that a physician
has expertise, and can with reasonable scientific
certainty predict possible outcomes. On the other hand,
a physician has no expertise in matters outside of
medicine, and thus cannot as readily identify or valuate
non-physiologic harm. In these matters, the valuation
must reside with the patient.[378]

When the issue is so framed, one needs to ask what
qualifies as "harm?" Hardly a clinical intervention occurs
that does not result in some clinical side-effect (mostly of
harmful nature), yet no one contests that administering
antihypertensive medication is unethical merely because
one of the side-effects is impotence (admittedly a harm to
most individuals).[379]   Thus, mere presence of a harm that
is possible or even inherent in a procedure cannot make
the performance of the procedure unethical. Only when
harms outweigh benefits, should a physician refrain from
acting. A balancing of harms and benefits must ensue
in order to determine whether a physician can ethically
participate in a certain course of action.

Before proceeding to an issue by issue consideration
of psychiatric involvement in the criminal justice system
in light of the above principle, a differentiation between
clinical and non-clinical harms[380] must be made. Clinical
harms are the physiologic consequences that result
from the treatment,[381] and are also known as side-
effects. A competent physician can make a judgment

on an individual basis whether the clinical benefits to a given patient outweigh the clinical harm to that patient.[382] In order to assess the different clinical harms and benefits, the physician can call on his training and education qua physician. It is within his area of expertise to evaluate whether a particular treatment will cause more physiologic damage than physiologic benefit and vice versa. It is because of that skill that a physician's assistance is sought in cases of illness. Therefore, in a situation where only considerations are of a clinical (physiological) nature, a physician, regardless of where and by who employed, can make a routine assessment of whether the benefits outweigh the harms, making it ethical to embark upon the course of treatment (subject to restrictions in Part V.A.2).

In the world of forensic psychiatry, however, there are also harms that can come about that are not physiologic, but that can be attributed to the physician's work. These extra-clinical harms, on the other hand, are much harder to quantify and calibrate with respect to any individual patient. What's more, it may be hard to even agree on what constitutes an extra-clinical harm. Even if it was possible to agree on what constitutes such extra-clinical harm, it is not readily apparent that physicians have any particular training or expertise to weigh these harms. Given these twin problems of identification and valuation of extra-clinical harms, it is much more difficult to arrive at a straight-forward formula for ethical behavior on the part of a physician. Nonetheless, extra-clinical harms must be taken into account and balanced against benefits prior to choosing a course of action; and the benefits of the action chosen must outweigh the harms. Although it is indeed difficult to define and valuate these harms, in the context of forensic psychiatry some extra-clinical harms are quite apparent.

It must also be emphasized that given the fact that the accused (or the condemned or the NGRI acquitted) is a patient of the forensic psychiatrist,[383] it is his interests that psychiatrist should take into account, and not those of the society at large. The patient's interests take primacy over whatever benefits society would derive from a different course of action. Because this is the standard that applies to the practice of medicine in the "free world" (i.e., in the world outside of criminal justice system), it should apply with equal force to the practice of medicine in another setting. With this in mind, the extra-clinical harms to the patient can now be identified.

Three main extra-clinical harms that stem from the interlacing of psychiatry and criminal justice system can be readily identified. First, and perhaps most obvious is the criminal incarceration of the individual. This qualifies as harm simply on the basis that incarceration is a punishment;[384] something unpleasant that one endures as a consequence of bad actions.

Second, the institutionalization at a mental hospital is also an extra-clinical harm. This is so for two reasons. Institutionalization restricts the freedom of the individual; it also gives rise to negative societal attitudes towards patients.[385] Stigma may also arise from a finding of insanity which does not trigger confinement in a mental institution. These harms are balanced against the benefits of medical help that one receives at the hospital and the benefits of not being incarcerated in prison as a result of the insanity finding. It is hard if not impossible to determine when these benefits outweigh the harms or vice versa, and thus a psychiatrist enters a very murky world indeed when his chosen course of action results in either of the outcomes.

The third harm that can arise from the involvement of psychiatrists in the penal process is the execution of the convicted individual. Unlike the incarceration, the execution is permanent, and unlike institutionalization, execution is not balanced by any benefits to the individual. (There may well be a societal benefit to executions, but that topic is best left for another article. Whatever benefit accrues to the society as a result of execution or other penal measures, is nonetheless irrelevant, for as discussed above, in a patient-physician interaction, the physician should be concerned about patient's harms and benefits not anyone else's.) Regardless, a physician does not act ethically when he uses his knowledge for purposes that are antithetical to healing, and nothing is more antithetical to healing then causing a death of an otherwise healthy human being.[386]

One can summarize the principle of "no harm" thus: a physician has to use his medical knowledge to determine whether or not clinical benefits outweigh clinical harms, and proceed only if they do. Physician must leave the weighing of non-clinical harms to the patient. In other words, no harm can be phrased as "no clinical harm."

TO MAKE any system of criminal justice work, it is necessary to presume that a person accused of an offense is innocent until proven guilty. We Americans are familiar with our right to be presumed innocent and are justly proud of it. But to make our system work, it is now also necessary that we presume that the defendant is psychiatrically fit to stand trial until proven otherwise. Although this assumption is just as important as the assumption about guilt or innocence, the public is unfamiliar with it and the media pay scant attention to it. Moreover, if our interest in the mental competence of the defendant is sincere, because we want to protect him from being tried unfairly, then we ought to be equally concerned, and for the same reason, about the competence of all of the dramatis personae in this morality play. Consider the following two scenarios.

SCENARIO 1: The defendant is a famous figure on trial for lying to Congress under oath and other sensational charges. The judge and the attorneys are seasoned courtroom performers. To protect the defendant's right to a fair trial, prospective jurors are asked whether they or any members of their families have been parties to or witnesses in any courtroom proceedings. One prospective juror, subsequently selected to serve, answers no. She is also asked whether she has heard of any of nearly two hundred people, among them the current President and his predecessor, and again she answers in the negative. After the trial we learn that one of her brothers had been convicted and served time for armed robbery. When questioned, she explains: "It left my mind because I didn't want to think about it . . . I forgot about it after I shed tears." She also forgot that two of her other brothers had also "been arrested at various times." Question: Was this person competent? Was the pre-trial interrogation intended to test her competence, and, if so, was her performance adjudged adequate to establish her fitness to serve as a juror?

SCENARIO 2: A man of no evident distinction or merit is accused of killing his wife by shooting her eight times with an assault rifle. After the shooting, he goes to a suburban airport, commandeers a small plane, flies over the city strafing the streets with gunfire, buzzes the control tower of the city's airport, forcing the workers to flee and close down the airport, and safely lands the plane. He is apprehended, charged, and ordered to undergo pre-trial psychiatric examination to determine his fitness to stand trial. In due course he is declared unfit, denying him his Sixth Amendment right to a speedy trial. Question: Which requires more mental competence: to perform the criminal acts described or to sit in a courtroom and be defended by one's attorney (assuming that the defendant prefers to be defended rather than punished as prescribed by law)? The evidence of this man's competence as a criminal--killing his wife, stealing a plane, shooting from it--is not contested and is open to public view. The evidence of his (alleged) lack of competence to be a defendant is arcane, hidden from public view, and in fact fabricated by "experts" to fit the desires of their employers.

These are, of course, not imaginary scenarios. The first is a thumbnail sketch of the Oliver North trial and the role of juror Tara Leigh King in it. The second is a thumbnail sketch of the deed of a gentleman named Alfred Hunter and the diversion of his case by Brockton (Massachusetts) District Court Judge Charles E. Black from the criminal-justice system to the psychiatric-"treatment" system. Note that in the North trial, a prospective juror who did not recognize the names of President Bush and former President Reagan (or answered the question about them mendaciously) was considered mentally competent to serve as a juror. If she was indeed that ignorant, then, no doubt, she wasn't "biased" about Mr. North. But if she was so "out of touch with reality" as not to know who the President is (a standard psychiatric-test question), how could she be competent to determine the legality or illegality of the defendant's conduct? On the other hand, an obscure man in an obscure courtroom whose pre-trial conduct was prima-facie evidence of a high level of mental competence was declared incompetent to act as a defendant.

IT IS TRUE, of course, that every role or task requires a different kind of competence: playing the piano one kind, playing tennis another. It is likewise with the different players in the courtroom. But this objection misses the point of my argument, which is this: We do not require that, as a condition of exercising the privilege of playing the role of judge, prosecuting attorney, defense attorney, or juror, the candidates for these roles first successfully pass a psychiatric examination; but we do require that, as a condition of exercising this constitutional right to trial, the defendant--the weakest, most defenseless, and only involuntary actor in the play-- successfully pass precisely such an examination.

I submit that we have been had. We zealously guard our horses from common thieves, white organized criminals, with more ambition and imagination, load the barn, horses and all, onto trucks and cart it off to their own corral. No one in American dreams of challenging the presumption that we are innocent until proven guilty, yet we guard it jealously; whereas the presumption that we are competent to stand trial--which had been ours from Colonial times until the middle of this century--we have slowly but surely relinquished to the mad-doctors and alienists, and no one seems alarmed or even aware of the loss.

Of all the actors in a courtroom drama, we question the psychiatric competence only of the defendant (typically only if he is charged with a so-called bizarre crime and usually only if he is a Very Unimportant Person who cannot defend himself against this tactic to disarm and disable him). But if we are truly interested in guaranteeing a defendant's right to a fair and speedy trial, should we not question the competence of all the actors? Or, better still, should we not assume that a person who is mentally capable of committing a sophisticated crime is, ipso facto, psychiatrically capable of standing trial for it and, if guilty, being punished for it?

2. The "Consent" Principle

As discussed above, the "no harm" principle has certain limitations, namely, the difficulty in identifying and valuating extra-clinical harm especially when balanced by a clinical benefit. Furthermore, "no harm" is not the end of the inquiry, as the sterilization example has shown. Thus, an additional step is needed to satisfy oneself that the action taken is indeed in the patient's interest.

The basic principle that ought to govern any medical intervention is that of personal autonomy. Personal autonomy is important for several reasons. First, it is consistent with the Kantian prohibition against using a person as a means. If a person is treated as nothing more than a mannequin that can be fine-tuned whenever something goes awry, then the individual is being used simply as a means to achieve a disease-free state. Therefore, a physician must take patient's desires into account before proceeding with any intervention. In this way, the person is being treated as an end, because any intervention is done not with the goal of promoting general well-being without reference to a specific individual, but with the goal of providing the patient with tools to achieve his own goals and live up to his own values.

Second, personal autonomy is important because of the difference in value preferences between a doctor and the patient.[387] It cannot be assumed that health and prolonged life are the top values for every individual.[388] Jehovah's Witnesses provide an excellent example. Although blood transfusion may save the life of a given individual, it will be refused by a Jehovah's Witness, because fidelity to religious tenets is a higher order value for that individual than health or life. For a physician it may be natural to elevate health to the top of the value rankings, as physician's life is dedicated to the preservation of health,[389] but for the patient, the rankings may be completely different. Thus, in order to keep the patient's value system intact, a physician should not act contrary to the patient's wishes.[390]

The patient himself must evaluate (after being provided with complete and truthful information) whether the benefits that any treatment will provide outweigh the harms inherent in such treatment.[391] Given the fact that medications used to treat mental illness often have significant harmful side-effects,[392] not to mention adverse extra-clinical consequences that arise out of being a confirmed mental patient, the individual should be allowed to judge for himself whether or not these negatives outweigh the positives of being under treatment.

"Value-preference" consent theory is also useful in resolving the problem of extra-clinical harm. As Part V.A.1 asserts, a physician has no expertise to perceive and quantify the extra-clinical harm that comes from interaction with the penal system versus, for example, the harm that comes from stigma of insanity label. To be sure, a physician can most certainly express his preference if he himself were in a similar situation, but that preference cannot substitute for the preference of the patient. Again then, consent is quite useful in resolving the dilemma of extra-clinical harm.

The above of course assumes a patient who is able to make decisions and give or withhold consent for procedures. A child, a person who lacks capacity to understand (e.g., someone with a low IQ score)[393] and a person who is so mentally ill as to not be able to process reality, are unable to weigh harms and benefits, and thus cannot consent to the procedure.[394] On the other hand, simply because consent cannot be obtained, it does not follow that no treatment should be provided. When a person cannot consent, a judgment must be made based on twin concepts of "best interest of the patient" [395] and the patient's own values, if known.[396]   When the physician is unaware of the patient's wishes, it has to be presumed that the patient would wish to be treated if such treatment comports with the "no harm" standard.

There is a caveat that must not go unaddressed. Whenever not treating an individual threatens harm to the society at large, the individual's rights deserve less deference than in a situation where society's interests [397] are not so threatened. [398] Thus, a person afflicted with tuberculosis has a right to be untreated on the condition that he is isolated from the rest of society. Similarly, a mentally ill patient who may be dangerous to himself or others, in principle retains his right to remain free of treatment if an alternative method of preventing harm to himself or society exists. However, if no alternative is present, a person must be treated to the point where the threat to himself or society is eliminated. However, once that point is reached, or an alternative is found, even if the person is not completely "cured," he regains his unqualified right to choose the scope and the amount of treatment for himself.

3. The "Professionalism" Principle

When one thinks of the Hippocratic Oath, one traditionally thinks of its proscription on causing harm. [399] However, the Oath also demands that a physician be loyal to his profession and that he keep his art pure. [400] Thus, whenever practicing medicine, a physician owes not only certain duties to his patient, but also a duty to his profession. Of course part of this "professional duty" is the requirement that the physician act in the best interest of the patient (according to the principles outline above), but that is not the whole of physician's responsibilities. He is also responsible for making sure that his actions, even if consonant with principles of "no harm" and "consent" are not harmful to the profession of medicine as a whole. That is not to say that in order to benefit the art and science of medicine one may harm a patient, but merely to say that prior to engaging in any action, a physician must consider both the effect on a given patient and the effect on the profession of medicine.

An objection to this principle can be raised along the lines that following the dictate of "professionalism" is no different from balancing harms to the patient against the harms to the society, an approach already rejected in this review.[401] Yet, this criticism is unwarranted. Unlike balancing patient's harms and benefits against that of the society, this principle does not call for the diminishing of the patient's central role in the risk-benefit analysis. Instead, this principle comes into play only when the "no harm" and "consent" principles have been satisfied.

Thus, a physician must first satisfy himself that no harm will come to the patient. If he cannot do so, the other two tests become irrelevant, for he should not take any action. If he can so satisfy himself, he must then proceed to elicit the patient's consent for the proposed action (subject to limitations outlined in Part V.A.2). Again, if the consent is denied, the physician must stop. If the consent is granted, the physician can proceed, but only insofar as the proposed actions will not reflect poorly on his profession.

As Part III mentions, [402] not all actions currently taken by psychiatrists are rooted in hard science. Aside from such questionable techniques as offering opinions based on nothing more than hypothetical questions propounded by counsel for either side,[403] psychiatrists also engage in actions for which they are simply not trained. Among them are predictions of future dangerousness, [404] and testifying on "test questions," which are nothing more than legal and moral conclusions.[405] Not being experts on the field, yet offering opinions on the matter, psychiatrists diminish their profession and bring it into disrepute. Because moral outlook (and thus testimony on issues of morality) by definition cannot be grounded in science, psychiatrist who do so testify practically invite opposing testimony. The "battle of the experts" that results often causes juries to discount psychiatric testimony altogether, [406] and diminishes the respect that the public holds for the profession.

B. Application of Principles

Bearing the above principles in mind one can review the participation of psychiatrists in the criminal justice system at points outlined in Part III, supra, a propos of these rules.

1. Competency to Stand Trial or for Execution

In evaluating the defendant prior to the beginning of trial so as to verify his mental state, the psychiatrists serves an essential medical function, one practiced by physicians the world over, namely assessing the patient. It is irrelevant who employs the physician, because as stated before, a physician "acting in a capacity that requires a psychiatrist's education, judgment, and experience is, in that role, practicing psychiatry," [407] and thus owes the primary duty of allegiance to the patient and not the employer. The potential conflict arises not in the actual evaluation,[408] but in submitting a report to the court detailing the findings. If the report is adverse to the defendant, an extra-clinical harm ensues, i.e., the defendant is brought to trial with the potential for conviction and incarceration.[409] On the other hand, if the report is favorable to the defendant, an extra-clinical harm ensues from the likely committal to a psychiatric institution with the attendant potential clinical harms from any medication that may be administered. Of course, with a favorable report, the defendant also enjoys the benefits (though perhaps temporary) of escaping criminal responsibility and/or punishment. At the very least, when the report is favorable to the defendant, harms are counter-balanced (though not necessarily outweighed) by the benefits. When the report is not favorable however, no such balancing occurs, and thus a psychiatrist causes more harm than good and becomes directly responsible for such harm.

Because a psychiatrist does not know a priori which way the competency report is going to come out, he runs the risk of placing himself in a situation where he would behave in an unethical manner. However, it cannot be that a psychiatrist can only be allowed to submit his report when such a report is beneficial to the patient. Another solution to this dilemma must exist. This solution must also close the door to the tendency of the courts to use psychiatric testimony at the competency stage as a justification to deal with the defendant in a way that they would have done anyway. Psychiatrists should not give in to the temptation to justify the decision of the courts, and should confine themselves to the proper medical function, i.e., evaluating a patient and providing medical information elicited from such evaluations for the court. Of course, a psychiatrist still cannot know a priori what medical information he will elicit from the patient exam, nor the way in which the court will treat the information. However, a psychiatrist can safely say that there are no identifiable harms that come from the examination itself, thus satisfying the first condition of ethical behavior.[410]   Second, a psychiatrist has the patient's consent for evaluation (or consent of someone standing in the stead of a presumably incompetent individual). However, that consent can only extend to the area within the psychiatrist's expertise. A psychiatrist can no more be presumed to have patient's consent to render legal opinions (and "competency" is a legal not medical matter), than he can be presumed to have patient's consent to invest in a stock market.

By solely engaging in a diagnostic procedure without drawing any legal conclusions therefrom, a psychiatrist escapes causing harm to the patient, and does not act beyond the scope of the consent. Whatever harm does result becomes attenuated by having been interpreted by and processed through the legal machinery.

One might ask how this solution is different from what occurs today. After all, a psychiatrist's report as to competency is not final; the final decision still remains with the court even under today's rules. The difference lies in the fact that today's rules allow the psychiatrist to pass on questions concerning the ultimate question,[411] i.e., is the defendant's mental health such that he cannot understand the charges against him or effectively assist in his own defense. Although the courts do have to pass the final judgment on the matter, they most often defer to the "expert" testimony.[412] The court-appointed psychiatrist for all intents and purposes becomes the final judge in determining whether the defendant will enter the criminal justice system, [413] and in that role he may end up behaving unethically in those cases where his determination causes harm without corresponding benefit to the patient. Being a "final judge" is medically unethical because it causes an identifiable harm to the patient, that is not balanced by any particular benefit, and because the psychiatrist is acting beyond his expertise and therefore, beyond the scope of consent.

Even assuming that the psychiatrist does have the patient's explicit consent to speak on moral issues, he should not do so, because it violates the "professionalism" principle. By testifying on issues of morality (presumably at patient's request), the psychiatrist invites opposing testimony from psychiatrist with different moral precepts. There will then be testimony cloaked in the legitimacy of the white coat, yet having nothing to do with either art or the science of medicine. Of course, lay populace may still feel resentful towards psychiatrists for "getting the defendant off," much in the same way that the feel resentment for attorneys who defend unpopular clients or causes. However, so long as psychiatrists do not stray from practicing medicine, i.e., from diagnosing and describing the diagnosis, such resentment will be minimal. In any case, whatever resentment there may be, it is inconsequential, for the science of medicine cannot be brought into disrepute simply because the legal profession chooses to use certain medical diagnosis as an exculpatory or mitigating factors.

The proposed solution would allow a psychiatrist to do nothing more than to document an illness from which the defendant may be suffering. In his report the psychiatrist would be allowed to list defendant's symptoms and diagnosis, as well as common patterns of behavior or problems exhibited by people with this diagnosis. He would also be allowed to state whether a given defendant encountered some, all or none of these problems. In other words, in court, the psychiatrist would act no differently than in a clinical setting where he would present the patient's case to a team of other psychiatrists. The court would then be presented with nothing more than medical testimony and would have to make its own judgment as to what to do with the defendant without using the "expert" testimony as a fig leaf. A psychiatrist, on the other hand, is spared venturing into potentially unethical terrain.

2. Testimony at Trial

The problem at a competency hearing is that the court generally relies on the court-appointed "independent" expert, and such expert does not know a priori whether his actions will cause more harm or more good, nor can he even make a good faith estimate on the issue, because he cannot properly valuate the harms. (That is markedly different from a physician embarking on a course of treatment that he is not sure will benefit his patient, for such physician at the very least has to have a good faith belief that the actions he takes are for the patient's overall physiologic benefit.) This problem is not present at trial when the issue of sanity at the time of the offense is litigated. The expert knows quite well what he is expected to testify to, simply based on who has hired him, and thus is aware of the patient's relative values of harms and benefits.[414] This of course is not to suggest that experts sell their testimony for money; nonetheless, it is clear that if an expert hired by either side does not confirm their theory, such expert will not be asked to testify.

Accordingly, the literal interpretation of the "no harm" principle would hold that psychiatrists testifying for the defense act ethically (because no harm comes from evaluation, and they act within the scope of the consent given, and consonant with the patient's value rankings when actually testifying), while those testifying for the prosecution do not (because they do not act consonant with the patient's value-rankings). This outcome cannot be right as a matter of policy calling for adversarial judicial process, where either side can use its experts to rebut the findings of experts for the other side. As a matter of ethics, however, it may very well be right. When a psychiatrist ventures onto the field of morals (and as discussed previously, Part II, supra, sanity is a matter of moral judgment) [415] he cannot claim the balance required in the legal system as a shield for his own actions; his actions must only be guided by the ethics of medicine, and not by any desires of the legal system. For that reason, when a psychiatrist chooses to testify for the prosecution, i.e., when he knowingly assists the state in its attempt to exercise its punitive power, he acts contrary to medical ethics.

It thus seems that good policy is in direct conflict with medical ethics so long as the current system is in place. However, by taking the approach enunciated in Part V.B.1, supra, i.e., limiting psychiatric testimony only to diagnosis and description of a recognized illness, the ethical quandary is avoided.[416] Diagnosis is a quintessentially medical function. Furthermore, medical diagnosis is grounded in science that can be agreed to by psychiatrists working for either the defense or the prosecution, while criminal responsibility is grounded in morals, and therefore susceptible to much broader disagreements. By simply adducing defendant's diagnosis (if any) into evidence, the psychiatrist does not directly help the state exercise its penal functions, for any decision as to how to interpret or how much weight to give to the defendant's diagnosis vis-à-vis his moral culpability remains the sole province of the court and the jury. By not drawing moral conclusions or answering "test questions," psychiatrists keep themselves away from the ethical morass of helping the state incarcerate or execute someone.

3. Actions of "Independent Panels"

This review has dedicated significant time and space to the discussion of an "independent panel" system of psychiatric involvement in the adjudicatory process. That discussion was to lay the groundwork for the argument that the ethical problems encountered by psychiatrists in the criminal justice system are not dependent on the adversarial system or the "battle of the experts;" [417] rather they result from the close involvement of psychiatrist in the criminal justice system. The Soviet system provided for an independent panel of experts to evaluate a defendant and pronounce his fitness to stand trial or his fitness to be held liable for his actions. Even though the psychiatrists technically were not there to help the state incarcerate individuals, given the fact that their decisions were rarely questioned, they exercised inordinate authority over the lives of human beings. The presence of that excess authority led to the numerous abuses of psychiatry.

Some may argue that it was the repressive Communist state that caused psychiatric abuses and not the vesting of power in the medical profession, but that argument is fallacious. The case of Colonel Budanov arose well after the collapse of the USSR, yet psychiatrists in that case were afforded significant opportunity to have the surrounding events and the political situation in the country influence their judgment. Granted, today's Russia is still far from the democratic ideals espoused by the United States; nonetheless, even in the United States, if given a completely free hand psychiatrists are likely to have their world outlook, current events and political persuasions color their judgment. It is at this point, when a psychiatrist overlays his own values onto a diagnosis, he perverts the medical nature of his involvement into a political and/ or penalogical tool. Such behavior is contrary to medical ethics, specifically, the principles of "no harm" and "professionalism," and should be guarded against. The solution to this problem is the one already discussed in the previous two subsections. With this solution adopted, a psychiatrist can only diagnose disease and his ability to impose his own values on that diagnosis is extremely limited. The problem of the Soviet-type system is solved not with cross-examination (although that too is highly useful and valuable) but limiting the range of testimony that psychiatrists can offer, thus shielding them from potentially unethical practices.

4. Medicating the Prisoners

Psychiatrists often have to medicate prisoners in order to maintain their mental health. The majority of such treatment is done with the defendant's consent and with no other purpose than to alleviate pain. These instances are fully consonant with the consent principle. However, as discussed is Part III, supra, there are instances when an incompetent person is medicated with the eye to make him competent to stand trial or be executed. The ethicist encounters two problems in this situation. One, if a person is incompetent and/or insane, and medicating him will restore his competence and/or sanity, a cognizable clinical benefit has been achieved, yet this benefit is balanced by an extra-clinical harm. The harm can be starkly defined, as in execution, or more amorphous, as in standing trial which may or may not result in punishment of varying severity. Second, because the person is incompetent, he cannot grant or withhold consent.[418]   Nor is relying on "the best interest of the patient" likely to provide any helpful guidance, for in order to define "best interests," one would need to balance harms and benefits, thus running into the problem of valuation and balancing already described. [419]   Faced with this predicament, a psychiatrist could simply decide to do what the legal system dictates, but such action would assume that what is legal is necessarily moral, hardly a self-evident proposition.

A middle ground is then perhaps the best and the only solution. A psychiatrist cannot allow himself to be the direct cause of death (or for that matter other punitive measures visited upon the prisoner). Thus, medicating someone solely for the purpose of restoring competence (be it for execution, trial, etc.) is wholly improper on the grounds of the "no harm" principle.[420]   It also violates the "consent" principle, as admittedly the purpose of medication is not to follow the patient's wishes, but simply to restore a legal status of competence. Yet, a psychiatrist cannot refuse to medicate a person on death row if a person wants to continue medication simply because such actions will keep that person competent and thus liable to be executed. This is so because a psychiatrist has to maintain his responsibility to the condemned as a patient, despite the fact that this patient is scheduled for execution. A physician's responsibility has to be uniform regardless of the patient's status in the criminal justice system. This responsibility is not a sliding scale where duty is inversely proportional to the level of restriction society has imposed on individual's freedom. Thus, the mere prospect of execution does not make psychiatric help unethical, any more than the fact of incarceration makes such help unethical. The dilemma must be resolved by resorting to patient's (prisoner's) own wishes. So long as the patient is informed of the consequences of his decisions, whether they result in the death penalty being applied, or in the prisoner languishing in a state of perpetual incompetence, or in any other outcome, the patient's wishes should be honored. In so doing, a psychiatrist acts within the canon of medical ethics.

The problem however, is that an incompetent inmate cannot consent to treatment. On the other hand, medicating such an individual cannot be said to be against his will, as the person does not have free will as a result of his own incompetence.[421]   Since medicating such an individual is likely to bring clinical relief without causing immediate death, it is then ethical for a psychiatrist to medicate such individual to competence. With restoration to competence, free will returns, and at that point, the prisoner may refuse further medication by exercising his free will and refusing to give his consent for further medication.

Operating under the principle of consent, a psychiatrist should then cease medicating the individual. Of course, once medication ceases, the prisoner is likely to revert back to the pre-medication condition, and it would be rather futile to have this process repeat ad infinitum. Fortuitously, no need for such repetition exists, for once the prisoner reverts back to incompetence, the psychiatrist must be guided by the principle of respecting patient's wishes previously expressed.

By acting according to the above scheme a psychiatrist maintains his duty to treat the ill, yet avoids being the instrument of death or other penal interests of the state. If the prisoner, after being restored to competence, judges that the harms of further treatment outweigh the benefits, he is free to cease treatment and thus bring to a halt all legal proceedings that the state has pending against him.

The main objection to this proposal will be the perception that some criminals will manipulate the system in such a way as to escape punishment. This review will not quarrel with this notion, but will provide an answer to the charge. Society has settled on the belief that the insane and incompetent are not fit for punishment. So long as this moral idea persists, society must live with the result that some people whom it would otherwise like to punish will be able to escape condemnation. Much like the society is willing to tolerate criminals taking refuge in the Fourth or Fifth Amendment to escape punishment no matter how strong the evidence of guilt is, so too must society accept the notion that so long as reprieve from punishment is available to the insane, some people would take refuge in it, even if they could be medicated out of their condition.

5. Treating the Acquitted

The same approach that was suggested towards prisoners should be taken towards the acquitted, for after all, those committed to psychiatric institutions differ from prisoners in name only. If the individual refuses treatment and constitutes a danger to himself or others, he can of course remain confined, and if he continues to constitute a threat even when confined, the exception to the consent principle can be invoked.[422] It is worth noting that even if the exception to the consent principle is invoked, one must recognize that the benefits (both clinical and extra-clinical) from such involuntary medication are quite tangible, while the harms are not; after all the patient no longer faces the threat of punishment within the criminal justice system, as he has already been acquitted.

The only additional point worth making is that psychiatrists must not let the judiciary dictate the methods of treatment to them. In Part III, supra, it has been mentioned that courts often ignore psychiatric recommendations as to patients who have been deemed worthy (in the clinical sense) of release from institutionalization.[423] While psychiatrists are powerless to challenge confinement orders, they cannot continue to carry out treatments that are no longer in the patient's interest. Such behavior would violate the "no harm" principle.[424] Thus, psychiatrists, if they wish to be involved in treating the NGRI acquitted, must treat them no different from other patients irrespective of the judicial views on this class of patients. In other words, judicial orders and power (e.g., deciding on commitment and release) cannot be used as a shield for psychiatrists engaging in an otherwise unethical behavior, i.e., acting contrary to the patient's interests.

6. Competency for Execution

A brief note must be made about psychiatric participation in execution. This article outlined the parameters of proper psychiatric involvement in trial competency evaluations in Part V.B.1. The argument here is that nothing changes when the hearing is to determine competency for execution as opposed to for trial. Although Professor Bloche argues that the death penalty is qualitatively different [425] from any other sort of punishment, it is argued here that the difference is only quantitative, and therefore does not require any special ethical consideration by psychiatrist. Whether a psychiatrist testifies in a setting of execution competency hearing, or pre-sentencing hearing, or pre-trial competency heating, legal consequences (of one sort or another) flow from such testimony. These legal consequences may be harmful to the individual about whose condition the testimony is being proffered. However, a psychiatrist is not in a position to evaluate these harms because he has no specialized training for doing so. Again, even if the patient consents to these harms, a psychiatrist must guard against unprofessional behavior.

The key therefore is to put as much of a distance as possible between physician's testimony and legal consequences of whatever sort, and to require a psychiatrist to act within the scope of the consent given him,[426] and within the scope of his professional expertise.[427]   This can be accomplished by the psychiatrist (regardless of who employs him) being no more than a physician to a given patient. He can therefore discuss the patient's medical condition but may not draw legal conclusions as to competency or "understanding." In short, in this setting, psychiatrist's duties to his patient are neither increased nor diminished, and he must act consistent with the principle of "no [medical] harm" and patient's consent.

7. To Trial

There should be no constitutional impediment to replacing the competency evaluation process with a system of trial continuances. Cases in which defendants seek to waive the incompetency doctrine and stand trial or plead guilty over an objection by the prosecution that they are incompetent represent only a small percentage of total cases. In the overwhelming majority of cases, it is the defendants, through their counsel, who raise the incompetency question as a bar to trial. Under existing practices, a formal competency evaluation is triggered by the defendant's request.

Instead of invoking the formal evaluation process in such cases, courts could grant a continuance of reasonable duration to the defendant based on the assertion of counsel that the defendant is incompetent.[428] This would require attorneys to certify that they seek the continuance in good faith and on reasonable grounds and to set forth the specific statements by the defendant that form the basis for the request. Counsel would have to support a request for a further continuance with a statement from a clinician certifying that the defendant was incompetent, stating that the defendant was receiving appropriate treatment, and predicting a restoration of the defendant's competence within a reasonable period.[429] The clinician's statement could also be required to include a specific treatment plan, detailing the kinds of treatment attempted and proposed. Defendants would get substantial choice in electing the type of treatment to improve their trial functioning. The place of treatment would depend on the defendant's bail status. If in custody, such treatment would be administered either in a jail or in a security mental health facility; if released, it would be administered in the community as an outpatient or voluntary inpatient. Defendants would bear the cost of treatment if not in custody, unless they were indigent.

In addition to avoiding the cost of unnecessary clinical evaluation and formal judicial determination of the defendant's competency, this proposal could have considerable therapeutic advantages for the defendant. Based on the literature on the psychology of choice,[430] the potential for successful treatment of defendants who are incompetent to stand trial is increased when the defendant accepts treatment voluntarily rather than when the defendant is coerced to enter a forensic facility.[431] Thus, placing the burden on the defendant (and counsel) to arrange for treatment with a provider of choice as a condition for receiving the requested continuance is both efficient and therapeutic. With active treatment, particularly treatment the defendant seeks to obtain, the great majority of mentally impaired defendants will gain sufficient competency to participate in trial within several weeks or months.[432]

Whereas, under existing practice, an incompetency determination suspends the criminal proceedings, the treatment continuance proposed here need not do so. During the continuance, the court could require the defense attorney to file any pretrial motions that can be resolved without the client's assistance.[433] Although the grant of a treatment continuance would suspend the defendant's right to a speedy trial, this scheme would permit defense counsel to file, at any time, a notice with the court that the defendant has become competent. Afterwards, proceedings should resume, with speedy trial periods again running.

Requiring certificates from counsel and from a clinician as conditions for the grant or renewal of a continuance, coupled with judicial supervision, should prevent abuse of the treatment continuance process. The trial judge maintains wide discretion over whether to grant or deny requested continuances,[434] and the judge could condition granting of a treatment continuance on receipt of weekly or monthly reports from the defendant's attorney or the treating clinician or both. The court would always be able to order an independent clinical evaluation or court-supervised treatment if necessary. The prosecutors would also monitor the process and could always move for a formal competency evaluation if they suspected abuse of the continuance process.[435]

The proposal that a defendant voluntarily accept treatment as a condition for the grant of a trial continuance could be joined with a form of "wagering" or behavioral contracting.[436] Under this proposal, to increase the efficacy of treatment, the defendant and the trial court could enter into a contingency contract under which the defendant would receive the continuance sought in exchange for an agreement to participate in an appropriate treatment program and for progressing toward the goal of restoration to competency, perhaps based on a specified schedule of target goals and dates culminating in a restoration to competency within a period specified in the contract. Jurisdictions could increase the incentive to perform effectively in treatment by denying the defendant credit against any ultimate sentence received for time spent in incompetency commitment unless the defendant makes a substantial effort.[437] In such jurisdictions, a credit against sentence could be used as a reinforcer in the contingency contract to induce an expeditious restoration to competency.[438]

Substituting a system of trial continuances for the existing formal incompetency process also would have the salutary effect of avoiding unnecessary incompetency labeling. As indicated, the term "incompetency to stand trial" has an unfortunate global and permanent connotation, implying an immutable impairment, rather than a temporary difficulty that in most cases is easily remedied.[439] The harmful psychological effects of using an incompetency label can be avoided by granting a "treatment continuance," a label that has no similar negative connotations. Even when it is necessary to make a formal incompetency determination, for example when defendants seek to waive a right that they are determined to be incompetent to waive, they could be found "temporarily impaired" or "temporarily unable to waive" the right in question.[440]   Such a label suggests hope rather than hopelessness, and encourages individuals to view their problem as one that appropriate treatment can resolve. Such a redesigned label would be less stigmatizing to defendants and would limit the risk that individuals might interpret their impairment as global and relatively stable, an attribution that would increase the likelihood of learned helplessness and other inhibitory patterns that interfere with a return to competency.[441]

8. Defining And Evaluating Competency In The Criminal Process

The Supreme Court adopted its classic formulation of the standard for incompetency in the criminal process in the 1960 case of Dusky v. United States.[442] The Court held that a court was required to determine whether the defendant "has sufficient present ability to consult with his lawyer with a reasonable degree of rational understanding and whether he has a rational as well as factual understanding of the proceedings against him." [443] Although some courts had applied a more demanding standard of competency when a defendant attempted to plead guilty or waive counsel (requiring the ability to make a reasoned choice), in Godinez v. Moran[444] the Supreme Court recently rejected such a higher standard. Instead, the Court found that the Dusky formulation was the appropriate test of competency throughout the criminal process.[445] The Dusky standard emphasizes the ability of a defendant to understand and consult, not necessarily the ability, to engage in rational decision-making. In Godinez, the Court distinguished between competency and the knowledge and voluntariness required for the waiver of certain fundamental rights.[446] A competency inquiry, the Court noted, focuses on the defendant's "mental capacity; the question is whether he has the ability to understand the proceedings."[447] By Contrast, the Court noted, the inquiry into "knowing and voluntary ... is to determine whether the defendant actually does understand the significance and consequences of a particular decision and whether the decision is uncoerced."[448]

Although the Court thus indicated that its competency standard was not as broad as some courts had thought, the standard is still quite broad, open-textured, and vague, permitting clinical evaluators substantial latitude in interpreting and applying the test.[449] The clinical instruments available for competency assessment compound the problem.[450] These instruments typically list the many potentially relevant capacities that a defendant might need without indicating which are most important.[451] Moreover, because clinical evaluators rarely consult with counsel to ascertain the particular skills the defendant will need to function effectively in a particular case, the assessment instruments, by listing a broad range of abilities, encourage clinical evaluators to apply a generalized, abstract standard of competency, rather than a more appropriate, contextualized approach to competency assessment.[452] By simply relying upon clinical judgment based upon all the circumstances, these instruments make competency assessment a highly discretionary exercise in clinical judgment.[453] In addition, many clinical evaluators are paternalistically oriented,

and, without more concrete guidance, tend to classify
marginally competent mental patients as incompetent.[454]
The literature documents the tendency of clinical
evaluations in the criminal courts to misunderstand
the legal issues involved in incompetency, frequently
confusing it with legal insanity or with the clinical
definition of psychosis.[455] Some clinicians over-diagnose
incompetency to bring about what seems to them a more
humane disposition of the case, or to secure mental
health treatment because they assume it will be helpful.[456]
The discretion vested in clinical evaluators is made
more troubling by the fact that appellate courts rarely
review, and almost never reverse, trial court competency
determinations,[457] and the fact that trial judges almost
always defer to clinical evaluators.[458]

Judicis officium est opus diei
in die suo preficere.

~

The role of a judge is to administer the law,
not to make it.

Chapter V

CONCLUSION

Insanity and criminal justice have been linked for over 2,000 years, and the involvement of psychiatrists in the criminal justice system both in the United States and abroad is here to stay. However, such involvement is fraught with ethical perils and can push a medical professional beyond the realm of treatment and cure and into the realm of punishment and execution. Such behavior is not consistent with the exalted role that the healers hold in society and tarnishes their role and image. What began as a noble attempt to have judges and juries render their verdicts on the basis of scientific evidence has too often deteriorated into psychiatrists being active participants in the state penal system. Such intertwining of two completely incompatible systems cannot continue if the ethics of the medical profession are to be maintained. In order to maintain the benefits of scientific information being available to the courts while upholding the principles of medical ethics, psychiatrists need to limit their involvement solely to scientifically verifiable information and act in the same way towards inmates that they would towards any other patient. With this approach there is yet a possibility that the high ethical standards demanded of healers will remain intact.

The existing competency process imposes substantial burdens on defendants and is extremely costly, yet a considerable number of defendants may, not require formal evaluation.

Empirical research on the costs of competency evaluation and treatment is almost non-existent. However, data from a study conducted ten years ago of costs in Dade County, Florida are useful as a rough basis for projecting national costs. Evaluation costs for an initial competency assessment averaged $2327, excluding court costs and the expense of an additional defense attorney, prosecutor, and judge time. These costs were based on evaluations. Inpatient evaluations for competency, still used in some jurisdictions, could easily double or even quadruple these Costs.41 Defendants found incompetent at this initial stage are hospitalized for several months of treatment, at an added average cost of $20,351. Thus, the total cost for a typical defendant found incompetent in Dade County exceeded $22,678. Costs for some cases ran considerably higher.

Using these Dade County figures, which are estimated to be low and are based on costs prevailing ten years ago, it can be estimated that in excess of $185 million is spent annually on competency evaluation and treatment in America. The costs today may be two or three times higher. With attorney and court costs included, the costs of the competency process nationally may exceed one billion dollars per year. Moreover, formal competency evaluations occur in many cases in which less formal screenings could suffice. Therefore, the competency determination results in a diversion of limited clinical resources that otherwise could be used for treatment.

The competency process also frequently imposes serious burdens on defendants. Prior to the Supreme Court's 1972 decision in Jackson v. Indiana, defendants hospitalized for treatment following a determination of incompetency to stand trial received what amounted to an indeterminate sentence of confinement in a mental hospital, typically for many years, often exceeding the maximum sentence for the crime charged, and sometimes lasting a lifetime. In Jackson, the Court recognized a constitutional limit on the duration of incompetency commitment, holding that a defendant committed solely based on trial incompetency cannot be held more than a reasonable period of time necessary to determine whether there is a substantial probability that he will attain that capacity in the foreseeable future." Any continued confinement, the Court held, must be based on the probability that the defendant would become competent within the foreseeable future. If the treatment provided does not advance the defendant toward competency, then the state must either institute customary civil commitment proceedings to detain the defendant, or release the defendant. Although Jackson marked an end to the most egregious cases of indefinite incompetency commitment, many states have responded insufficiently to the Court's decision, and abuses persist.

Lengthy incompetency commitment is particularly burdensome for defendants charged with misdemeanors - perhaps a majority of those found incompetent. If convicted, many of these defendants would pay a small fine or receive a period of probation. Instead, they might spend months or years confined as incompetent. Many of the hospitals in which defendants are confined are maximum security institutions that are poorly funded and staffed.51 Although many states now authorize outpatient treatment for trial incompetency, most defendants found incompetent are hospitalized. Such hospitalization is frequently unnecessarily restrictive of defendant's liberty and stigmatizing. In some jurisdictions, even where forensic hospitalization is not prolonged, other abuses occur. Those jurisdictions use short-term commitment based on incompetency to stand trial as an alternative to ordinary civil commitment. In misdemeanor cases, these defendants often will be released after several months with their charges dismissed. However, even this period of hospital confinement may be unnecessary, may not satisfy state commitment criteria, and will be more restrictive and less therapeutic than typical civil hospitalization.

The incompetency determination also imposes a serious stigma on defendants labeled incompetent to stand trial. Although these defendants already bear the stigma of a criminal accusation, the added stigma of being labeled incompetent may be considerably worse. Moreover, these defendants are further stigmatized by being associated with the often-notorious institutions to which they are committed - high security mental health correctional facilities like Dannamoura, Bridgewater, or Ionia - that evoke in the public imagination an image of the dangerously mad.

The label "incompetent" also has an unfortunate general and global connotation that may make defendants feel not only that they are unfit to stand trial, but also that they are incompetent to do anything. Moreover, the "incompetent" label suggests a permanent deficit, rather than a temporary impairment. Individuals so labeled may come to think that their difficulties cannot be helped. This can impede successful treatment. Imposition of an incompetency label, therefore, can be extremely debilitating to the individual. Many criminal defendants already have problems that they feel are beyond their control. Labeling these defendants incompetent, particularly against their will, can foster what Martin Seligman called "learned helplessness." This syndrome, characterized by generalized feelings of helplessness, hopelessness, depression, and lack of motivation, mirrors the symptoms of clinical depression.

Endnotes

1   Matthew 22:21 (American Standard Version)

2   See generally, JUDITH NEAMAN, SUGGESTIONS OF THE DEVIL: INSANITY IN THE MIDDLE AGES AND THE TWENTIETH CENTURY (Anchor ed. 1975).

3   For example, Chinese law also allowed the mentally ill to escape punishment for their criminal acts. See, e.g., Robin Munro, Judicial Psychiatry in China and its Abuses, 14 COLUM. J. ASIAN L. 1, 15-18 (2000).

4   See NEAMAN, supra note 2, at 67-68.

5   Throughout this article, for the sake of brevity and consistency the term "psychiatry" or "psychiatrist" is used; however, it is meant to encompass all mental health professionals.

6   See Michael L. Perlin, Unpacking the Myths: The Symbolism Mythology of Insanity Defense Jurisprudence, 40 CASE W. RES. L. REV. 599, 674 (1989/1990) ("This tragic ambivalence is reflected in judicial desires to have mental health experts testify as to future dangerousness, an expertise which psychiatrists themselves freely acknowledge they do not have, and to have them "take the weight" on difficult decisions involving commitment or release, especially in the cases of individuals hospitalized following insanity acquittals").

7   For a general discussion on the rules and stages of psychiatric involvement in criminal justice system see WAYNE R. LAFAVE, CRIMINAL LAW (3rd ed.) 363-391 (2000); see also ABRAHAM S. GOLDSTEIN, THE INSANITY DEFENSE (1967).

8   See, e.g., CRIMINAL RESPONSIBILITY AND PSYCHIATRIC TESTIMONY, COMMITTEE ON PSYCHIATRY AND THE LAW, GROUP FOR ADVANCEMENT OF PSYCHIATRY (May 1954) in BY REASON OF INSANITY (Lawrence Z. Freedman ed. 1983) 12 (stating that psychiatric testimony is "in the interest of a comprehensive criminal justice.")

9   See generally LAFAVE, supra note 8; GOLDSTEIN, supra note 8.

10   See generally LAFAVE, supra note 8, at 368.

11   See GOLDSTEIN, supra note 8, at 134.

12   Henry Weihofen, Eliminating the Battle of the Experts in Criminal Insanity Cases, 48 MICH. L. REV. 961,962 (1950). (Hereinafter Battle of the Experts).

13   See id. at 967. (Suggesting that juries tend to disbelieve "experts" if they also have an access to "independent" opinion.)

14   Ledger Wood, Responsibility and Punishment, 28 J. CRIM. L. & CRIMINOLOGY 630, 639 (1939).

15   John J. Diulio, Jr., Prisons are a Bargain, By Any Measure, N.Y. TIMES, Jan. 16, 1996 at A17

16   The insane cannot be deterred by punishment because as a result of mental illness they do not respond as expected to societal stimuli. See GOLDSTEIN, supra note 8, at 13.

17   See supra note 33 and the accompanying text.

18   GOLDSTEIN, supra note 8, at 13.

19   LAFAVE, supra note 8, at 326.

20   Id. at 382.

21   See generally NEAMAN, supra note 2.

22   Idiocy was considered to be an inborn and hereditary condition, akin to what today would be called mental retardation. Idiots could never achieve normalcy, and therefore never had either rights or responsibilities commensurate with that of the rest of the citizenry. See JOHN BRYDALL, NON COMPOS MENTIS, OR THE LAW RELATING TO NATURAL FOOLS, MADFOLK, AND LUNATICK PERSONS, INQUISITED, AND EXPLAINED FOR COMMON BENEFIT 6 (1700).

23   Lunacy, unlike idiocy, was not considered to be either inborn or hereditary. A lunatic could have moments of "clarity" whereupon all rights and responsibilities of a citizen would devolve upon him (until the relapse). See id. at 94; see also HENRICI DI BRACTON, DE LEGIBUS ET CONSUETUDINIBUS ANGLIAE [ON LAWS AND CUSTOMS OF ENGLAND] 321 (Travers Twiss, ed. & trans., William S. Hein & Co., Inc. 1990) (1250).

24   See NEAMAN, supra note 2. (The law cared not about the

diagnosis, but whether the defendant could behave in accordance with the law).

25 See id.

26 ANTHONY FITZHERBERT, NATURA BREVUM 579 (1534).

27 See NEAMAN, supra note 2.

28 See BRYDALL, supra note 49, at 12..

29 Id. At 110.

30 NEAMAN, supra note 2, at 77.

31 Id. at 68-69.

32 See Fran R. Freemon, The Origin of Medical Expert Witness, 22 J. LEGAL MED. 349 (2001).

33 Although there were insanity defenses and acquittals before that time, this trial is one of the few that occurred quite a long time ago, and yet is very well documented. Furthermore, even though there were such pleas and acquittals, up until 1740 they were quite few in number, and perhaps this contributed to lack of documentation. See Richard Moran, The Origin of Insanity as a Special Verdict: The Trial for Treason of James Hadfield (1800), 19 LAW & SOC'Y REV. 487, 488 (1985). Furthermore, it must be noted that juries relied mostly on their personal understanding of sanity and insanity, and although medical experts testified their testimony was given no more or less credence than testimony of any other person. Freemon, supra note 58, at 349.

34 Trial of James Hadfield For High Treason, 27 Howell's English State Trials 1281 (K.B. 1800).

35 Id. at 283.

36 Moran, supra note 60, at 496-497.

37 27 How. St. Tr. at 1330.

38 Id.

39 Moran, supra note 60, at 504.

40 27 How. St. Tr. at 1281.

41 See Moran, supra note 59, at 502-08.

42 See 27 How. St. Tr. 1330-56.

43   See id. at 1332-36.

44   Id. at 1332-33.

45   Id. at 1334.

46   Id. at 1335.

47   See generally Perlin, supra note 7; see also NEAMAN, supra note 2.

48   See NEAMAN, supra note 3, at 69.

49   The major underlying reason for administering punishment on an individual basis is a belief in personal responsibility. See Francis B. Sayre, Mens Rea, 45 HARV.L.REV. 974 (1932).

50   See GOLDSTEIN, supra note 8, at 12-13.

51   A famous experiment by a Russian physiologist Ivan Pavlov showed that a dog can be conditioned to exhibit a physiological response based on an unrelated stimulus that is paired with a stimulus that naturally causes the said physiological response.

52   See GOLDSTEIN, supra note 8, at 12.

53   Id. at 12-13.

54   LAFAVE, supra note 8, at 326.

55   MICHAEL MOORE, LAW & PSYCHIATRY: RETHINKING THE RELATIONSHIP 234 (1984).

56   Id.

57   This follows from the underlying premise of the theory that when causes of bad behavior are removed, the delinquent will act right. LAFAVE, supra note 8, at 24. Incarceration, irrespective of the amount of training for the new life that it provides, simply cannot cure a medical condition, so the insane even with the new skills the insane will not be able to act "right." Cf. Helen H. Stern, Madness in the Criminal Law, 40 TEMPLE L.Q. 348, 360 (1967).

58   FRANKLIN ZIMRING, PERSPECTIVES ON DETERRENCE 4 (1971).

59   HEINRICH OPPENHEIMER, THE RATIONALE OF PUNISHMENT 293-94 (1913).

60   ZIMRING, supra note 26, at 3.

61 Id.

62 Sometimes it is referred to as retribution or revenge or retaliation. LAFAVE, supra note 7, at 26.

63 IMMANUEL KANT, THE PHILOSOPHY OF LAW 195 (W. Hastie tr. 1887)

64 See JAMES F. STEPHEN, A HISTORY OF CRIMINAL LAW OF ENGLAND 81 (1883).

65 See MICHAEL S. MOORE, THE MORAL WORTH OF RETRIBUTION IN RESPONSIBILITY CHARACTER AND EMOTIONS (F. Shoeman, ed.) 179 (1987).

66 LAFAVE, supra note 8, at 24.

67 Ledger Wood, Responsibility and Punishment, 28 J. CRIM. L. & CRIMINOLOGY 630, 639 (1939).

68 John J. Diulio, Jr., Prisons are a Bargain, By Any Measure, N.Y. TIMES, Jan. 16, 1996 at A17.

69 The insane cannot be deterred by punishment because as a result of mental illness they do not respond as expected to societal stimuli. See GOLDSTEIN, supra note 8, at 13.

70 See supra note 33 and the accompanying text.

71 GOLDSTEIN, supra note 8, at 13.

72 Id.

73 Punishing people who are not viewed to be "blameworthy" does not educate anyone on anything, instead it blurs distinctions between culpable, and non-culpable conduct. LAFAVE, supra note 8, at 326.

74 One is not deterred if he cannot identify with the situation of the criminal. As most individuals cannot identify with the mentally ill, the punishment does not deter. GOLDSTEIN, supra note 8, at 13.

75 See supra note 40.

76 GOLDSTEIN, supra note 8, at 12.

77 LAFAVE, supra note 8, at 326.

78 Id. at 382.

79 See The Insanity Defense: ABA and APA Proposals for Change, 7 MENTAL DISABILITY REP. 136, 141 (1983).

80   See generally NEAMAN, supra note 2.

81   Idiocy was considered to be an inborn and hereditary condition, akin to what today would be called mental retardation. Idiots could never achieve normalcy, and therefore never had either rights or responsibilities commensurate with that of the rest of the citizenry. See JOHN BRYDALL, NON COMPOS MENTIS, OR THE LAW RELATING TO NATURAL FOOLS, MADFOLK, AND LUNATICK PERSONS, INQUISITED, AND EXPLAINED FOR COMMON BENEFIT 6 (1700).

82   Lunacy, unlike idiocy, was not considered to be either inborn or hereditary. A lunatic could have moments of "clarity" whereupon all rights and responsibilities of a citizen would devolve upon him (until the relapse). See id. at 94; see also HENRICI DI BRACTON, DE LEGIBUS ET CONSUETUDINIBUS ANGLIAE [ON LAWS AND CUSTOMS OF ENGLAND] 321 (Travers Twiss, ed. & trans., William S. Hein & Co., Inc. 1990) (1250).

83   See NEAMAN, supra note 2. (The law cared not about the diagnosis, but whether the defendant could behave in accordance with the law).

84   See id.

85   ANTHONY FITZHERBERT, NATURA BREVUM 579 (1534).

86   See NEAMAN, supra note 2.

87   See BRYDALL, supra note 49, at 12.

88   Id. at 110.

89   NEAMAN, supra note 2, at 77.

90   Id. at 68-69.

91   See Fran R. Freemon, The Origin of Medical Expert Witness, 22 J. LEGAL MED. 349 (2001).

92   Although there were insanity defenses and acquittals before that time, this trial is one of the few that occurred quite a long time ago, and yet is very well documented. Furthermore, even though there were such pleas and acquittals, up until 1740 they were quite few in number, and perhaps this contributed to lack of documentation. See Richard Moran, The Origin of Insanity as a Special Verdict: The Trial for Treason of James

Hadfield (1800), 19 LAW & SOC'Y REV. 487, 488 (1985). Furthermore, it must be noted that juries relied mostly on their personal understanding of sanity and insanity, and although medical experts testified their testimony was given no more or less credence than testimony of any other person. Freemon, supra note 58, at 349.

93   Trial of James Hadfield For High Treason, 27 Howell's English State Trials 1281 (K.B. 1800).

94   Id. at 283.

95   Moran, supra note 60, at 496-497.

96   How. St. Tr. at 1330.

97   Id.

98   Moran, supra note 60, at 504.

99   27 How. St. Tr. at 1281.

100   See Moran, supra note 59, at 502-08.

101   See 27 How. St. Tr. 1330-56.

102   See id. at 1332-36.

103   Id. at 1332-33.

104   Id. at 1334.

105   Id. at 1335.

106   Mr. Lidderdale was an army surgeon with the 15th Light Dragoon Regiment, the same one that Hadfield served in. 27 How. St. Tr. at 1135.

107   Id. at 1335-36.

108   See supra notes 59-60 and accompanying text.

109   Moran, supra note 60, at 506.

110   LAFAVE, supra note 8, at 378.

111   See, e.g., State v. Armant, 719 So.2d 510 (La. App. 1998); Holt v. State, 181 P.2d 573 (Okl. App. 1947). But see State v. Doiron 90 So. 920 (La. 1922) (holding that a physician, who had no knowledge or experience with mental diseases or insane persons, was not competent to testify as an expert on insanity).

112   See Weihofen, Battle of the Experts, supra note 13, at 966-
        67.

113   See supra notes 58-59 and 75 and accompanying text.

114   Scott E. Sundby, The Jury As Critic: Empirical Look at How
        Juries Perceive Expert and Lay Testimony, 83 VA. L. REV. 1109
        (1997).

115   E.g., State v. Evans, 523 A.2d 1306 (Conn. 1987); Montano
        v. State, 468 N.E.2d 1042 (Ind. 1984); Ice v. Commonwealth,
        667 S.W.2d 671 (Ky. 1984); Commonwealth v. Tyson, 402 A.2d
        995 (Pa. 1979).

116   See supra, note 82 and accompanying text.

117   Jurors tend to view conflicting experts as essentially canceling
        each other out, thus negating the very benefits that experts
        are supposed to provide. See Sundby, supra note 82, at 1138-
        39.

118   See supra, notes 4 and 14-15 and accompanying text.

119   BRACTON, supra note 50, at 321.

120   See Perlin, supra note 7, at n. 140.

121   Id.

122   See NIGEL WALKER, CRIME AND INSANITY IN ENGLAND 28-
        29 (1973).

123   See, e.g., Atkins v. Virginia, 536 U.S. 304 (2002) (holding the
        execution of mentally retarded unconstitutional); Ford v.
        Wainwright, 477 U.S. 399 (1986) (holding unconstitutional the
        execution of the insane); see also 18 U.S.C. [section] 3596(c)
        (exempting the mentally retarded from death penalty); Ga.
        Code Ann. [section] 17-7-131(j) (same); N.Y. Crim. Proc. Law
        [sections 400.27 (same).

124   See Pelin supra note 7, at 631-40.

125   16 How. St. Tr. 695 (1724).

126   Id.

127   Raymond L. Spring, Farewell to Insanity: A Return to Mens
        Rea, 66-MAY J. KAN. B. ASS'N. 38, 39 (1997).

128   The "right and wrong" or "wild beast" tests were in essence
        "all-or-none." If a person could exhibit some reason no matter

how small, he would generally be considered competent. See Brydall, supra note 49, at 8 (stating that if a person can name the days of the week or count to twenty, or know his age or know who his parents are, he is not an "idiot.").

129   See supra notes 60-75 and accompanying text.

130   See supra note 60.

131   M'Naghten's Case, 8 Eng. Rep. 718 (1843).

132   Id at 722.

133   Id.

134   Indeed the first wholesale revision occurred in 1954 when a new legal test for insanity was proposed. See infra notes 103-06 and accompanying text. It must be said though that in 1929 in Smith v. United States, 36 F.2d 548 (1929), the D.C. Circuit added "irresistible impulse" as an additional excuse.

135   See infra notes 113-15 and accompanying text.

136   214 F.2d 862 (D.C. Cir. 1954), overruled by U. S. v. Brawner, 471 F.2d 969, 981 (D.C.Cir. 1972).

137   214 F.2d at 872.

138   Id, at 874-75.

139   Id.

140   See id. at 875.

141   See id.

142   Id. at 876.

143   Id.

144   214 F.2d at 876.

145   U. S. v. Brawner, 471 F.2d 969, 981 (D.C.Cir. 1972).

146   For example, the United States follow M'Naghten rule, 18 U.S.C. [section] 20, while many states have adopted the ALI Model Penal Code definitions either by statute or court decision. See, e.g., Commonwealth v. Sheehan, 383 N.E.2d 1115 (Mass. 1978); State v. Johnson, 399 A.2d 469 (R.I. 1979); Graham v. State, 547 S.W.2d 531 (Tenn. 1977); State v. Grimm 195 S.E.2d 637 (W.Va. 1973). See also, John Ogloff, A Comparison of Insanity Defense Standards on Juror Decision Making, 15 L. & HUMAN BEH. 509, 510 (1991).

147   See Valerie P. Hans & Dan Slater, John W. Hinckley, Jr. & the Insanity Defense: The Public Verdict, 47 PUB. OPINION Q. 202 (1983).

148   MODEL PENAL CODE [section] 4.01.

149   The Model Penal Code stated that the whether defendant had "knowledge" of right and wrong cannot be answered by science, and is better left to the province of theologians and philosophers. Id., [section] 4.01, Appendix A (1985).

150   M'Naghten's Case, 8 Eng. Rep. 718, 722 (1843).

151   MODEL PENAL CODE [section] 4.01 (1).

152   See, e.g., Richard H. Kuh, The Insanity Defense--An Effort to Combine Law and Reason, 110 U. PA. L. REV. 771,797-99 (1962).

153   Cf. id. at 799.

154   See supra notes 87-121 and the accompanying text.

155   course some jurisdictions also deem it to be too lenient. See supra note 114-15 and accompanying text.

156   See, e.g., Durham, 214 F.2d at 870-71.

157   See supra note 78 and accompanying text.

158   See generally, M. Gregg Bloche, Psychiatry, Capital Punishment, and the Purposes of Medicine, 16 Int'l. J. L. & Psychiatry 301, 311-16 (1993) (hereinafter Psychiatry and Capital Punishment).

159   Id. at 311.

160   Id. at 312.

161   See id. at 314.

162   LAFAVE, supra note 8, at 382.

163   Weihofen, Battle of the Experts, supra note 13, at 277-78.

164   Id. at 279-80.

165   Id. at 280-83. This technique, largely due to its inherent flaws, however is not frequently used. LAFAVE, supra note 8, at 378.

166   See WILLIAM A. WHITE, INSANITY AND THE CRIMINAL LAW 86 (1923); Weihofen, Battle of the Experts, supra note 13, at 283; L. Vernon Briggs, Medico-Legal Insanity and the

Hypothetical Question 14 J. CRIM. L. & CRIMINOLOGY 62 (1923).

167 Some states have statutes requiring the state to pay for the psychiatric defense of the indigents. See Ake v. Oklahoma, 470 U.S. 68, 79 n. 4 (1985). In Ake, the Court recognized that psychiatric evaluation may be necessary for the defense to properly present its case and required states to provide a psychiatrist for that purpose. Although the Court did not explicitly say that the psychiatrist must work exclusively for the defense (i.e., implying that prosecution and defense can "share"), the Court did recognize that psychiatrists disagree widely and frequently" on the issue of legal insanity. This may imply that "sharing" will not work, as defense and prosecution will each seek out psychiatrists with differing points of view. Id. at 80-81. Based on the foregoing some have concluded that a "partisan" expert is constitutionally required. E.g., John M. West, Expert Services and the Indigent Criminal Defendant: The Constitutional Mandate of Ake v. Oklahoma, 84 MICH. L. REV. 1326, 1346 (1986).

168 See Ake, 407 U.S. at 81-82.

169 See supra notes 115-19 and accompanying text.

170 E.g., Weihofen, Battle of the Experts, supra note 13; see also Thomas Mackey (unpublished manuscript on file with the author).

171 See, e.g., MARGARET A. HAGEN, WHORES OF THE COURT: THE FRAUD OF PSYCHIATRIC TESTIMONY AND THE RAPE OF AMERICAN JUSTICE (1997); see also ALAN DERSHOWITZ, THE ABUSE EXCUSE AND OTHER COP OUTS, SOB STORIES, AND EVASIONS OF RESPONSIBILITY 38 (1994) (calling psychiatric testimony "psychobabble").

172 See, e.g., HENRY WEIHOFEN, MENTAL DISORDER AS A CRIMINAL DEFENSE 286 (1954). (Hereinafter, CRIMINAL DEFENSE); Cf. People v. Jones, 266 P.2d 38 (Cal. 1954) (allowing psychiatric testimony on issue of defendant's character because it can help in determining whether one was a "sexual deviant").

173 See infra note 192 and accompanying text.

174   Bloche, Psychiatry and Capital Punishment, supra note 126, at 311; Jeffrey A. Wertkin, Competency to Stand Trial, 90 GEO. L. J. 1514, 1517 (2002).

175   Joanmarie I. Davoli, Still Stuck in the Cuckoo's Nest: Why Do Courts Continue to Rely on Antiquated Mental Illness Research? 69 TENN. L. REV. 987,995-96 (2002).

176   Dusky v. U.S., 362 U.S. 402 (1960) (per curiam).

177   See Jackson v. Indiana, 406 U.S. 715, 717 n. 1 (1972) (quoting Indiana statute dealing with incompetence to stand trial. IND. CODE [section] 35-5-3-2 (1971)).

178   Indeed it is this procedure that gave rise to Jackson's complaint. Id. at 719.

179   406 U.S. 715 (1972).

180   Id. at 738. Confinement however often does last significantly longer than the bare minimum required to make a judgment on the issue. Nonetheless, essentially perpetual pretrial confinement is no longer practiced.

181   See LAFAVE, supra note 8, at 368.

182   See generally id.

183   See supra, note 106 and accompanying text.

184   See GOLDSTEIN, supra note 8, at 131-36.

185   See id. at 132.

186   LAFAVE, supra note 8, at 368.

187   Id.

188   See, e.g., Bruce J. Winick, Restructuring Competency to Stand Trial, 32 UCLA L. REV. 921, 930 -32 (1985) (suggesting that the majority of evaluations are still done on inpatient basis); Rodney J. Uphoff, The Role of the Criminal Defense Lawyer in Representing the Mentally Impaired Defendant: Zealous Advocate or Officer of the Court?, 1988 WIS. L. REV. 65, 71 n. 3 (1988). But see W. Lawrence Fitch & Susan R. Steinberg, Competency to Stand Trial and Criminal Responsibility, 36-FEB. MD. B. J. 14, 18 (2003) (stating that in Maryland defendants first undergo a "screening evaluation" and only if there are any questions after such evaluation, an inpatient observation is ordered).

189   GOLDSTEIN, supra note 8, at 131.

190   Id. 131-36.

191   LAFAVE, supra note 8, at 372.

192   Weihofen, Battle of the Experts, supra note 13, at 967-68.

193   See GOLDSTEIN, supra note 8, at 132-33.

194   See C.R. JEFFERY, CRIMINAL RESPONSIBILITY AND MENTAL DISEASE 159 (1st 1967); LAFAVE, supra note 7, at 363 ("It is to the advantage of both prosecutor and the defense to have the defendant examined by a psychiatrist whose orientation and examination procedures are such as will probably support their side of the case."); Cf. GOLDSTEIN, supra note 8, at 134 (stating that psychiatrist's own views on theory of psychiatry as a science play (or should play) an important role in him being selected or not selected as a witness for a given side.)

195   ABRAHAM L. HALPERN, USE AND MISUSE OF PSYCHIATRY IN COMPETENCY EXAMINATION OF CRIMINAL DEFENDANTS, IN PSYCHIATRISTS AND THE LEGAL PROCESS: DIAGNOSIS AND DEBATE 104 (Richard J. Bonnie ed. 1977).

196   Id. at 105.

197   Id.

198   Davoli, supra note 143, at 995-96.

199   See JUSTIN W. POLIER, THE RULE OF LAW AND THE ROLE OF PSYCHIATRY 15 (1968).

200   Id.

201   Bloche, Psychiatry and Capital Punishment, supra note 126, at 312.

202   GOLDSTEIN, supra note 8, at 124.

203   Id. 103-04.

204   This is due to the fact that at the "competence" stage the defendant is often examined by a court appointed, "independent" psychiatrist whose opinion carry great weight. See supra notes 152-60 and the ac

205   As can be expected, the psychiatrist's expertise is in medical issues of mental illness. The jury however has to come to a legal conclusion as to responsibility. Thus, whenever a

psychiatrist is asked questions, issues such as "whether the defendant was responsible" or "could appreciate his actions," he is rendering an opinion on a legal issue while armed only with medical expertise.

206   GOLDSTEIN, supra note 8, at 97.

207   Id.

208   See, e.g., FED.R. EVID. 704(b); United States v. Hillsberg, 812 F.2d 328, 331-32 (7th Cir. 1987); United States v. Felak, 831 F.2d 794, 797 (8th Cir. 1987).

209   Nowadays, psychiatrists can testify as to sanity, and also answer "test questions," thus in essence rendering the prohibition on "ultimate question" testimony toothless. See infra, notes 178-87 and accompanying text.

210   See Bryant v. State, 13 S.E.2d 820 (1941).

211   See, e.g., State v. McCann, 47 S.W.2d 95 (1932).

212   LAFAVE, supra note 8, at 378.

213   See GOLDSTEIN, supra note 8, at 98. ([The expert] would be permitted to answer only 'questions upon the matter of science.'")

214   Id. at 99.

215   See, e.g., MODEL PENAL CODE [section] 4.07(4).

216   LAFAVE, supra note 8, at 378.

217   MODEL PENAL CODE [section] 4.07(4).

218   See WEIHOFEN, CRIMINAL DEFENSE, supra note 140, at 286 (1954).

219   If the experts were to come to the same conclusion the need for trial would be obviated, as prosecution is unlikely try a case where the defendant would be pronounced insane even by the state expert. Alternatively, if the defense expert found the defendant sane, the counsel for the defense is unlikely to call such expert to the stand.

220   GOLDSTEIN, supra note 8, at 103-04.

221   This presumption must hold because otherwise one must conclude that the psychiatric testimony is of no value whatever.

222   Granted, in most instances NGRI acquitted are civilly confined. See infra, notes 246-77 and the accompanying text. However, the possibility does exist that such release will occur.

223   See supra, notes 113-14 and the accompanying text.

224   The very definition of a valid scientific experiment is that it is reproducible. If one cannot come to the same result using the same data, the experiment is not considered valid.

225   Ford v. Wainwright, 477 U.S. 399 (1986).

226   It is not for this article to debate whether all, some or none of these claims of incompetence are genuine. What this article does suggest that given the stakes, it is possible and indeed desirable (from the point of view of the condemned) to attempt to manipulate the system, and enlist help of the psychiatrist in the process.

227   See Bloche, Psychiatry and Capital Punishment, supra note 126, at 311-16.

228   Id. at 305-10.

229   Id. at 305.

230   Id. at 306.

231   Id.

232   Id. Although competency for execution may not be the same as competency to stand trial, given the very low threshold for the former, one is likely to satisfy it if one is competent to stand trial. See Ford v. Wainwright, 477 U.S. 399, 421 (Powell, J., concurring) (stating that one is competent for execution if one has "awareness of the penalty's existence and purpose"). It seems that this is a less demanding standard then competency for trial where one needs to be not only aware of the proceedings, but be able to understand them.

233   Bloche, Psychiatry and Capital Punishment, supra note 126, at 306.

234   Id.

235   Id. This is not to say that these procedures met the requirements later announced in Ford. Nonetheless, the states did undertake a separate evaluation of the condemned.

236   The actual procedural requirements are quite unclear.

Although Ford v. Wainwright, did hold that executing the incompetent is not constitutionally permissible, and required that the prisoner be heard on the issue, the parameters of the hearing are unclear. See LAFAVE, supra note 8, at 362.

237 Bloche, Psychiatry and Capital Punishment, supra note 126, at 306.

238 477 U.S. 399.

239 See, e.g., Solesbee v. Balkcom, 339 U.S. 9, 11-12 (1950) (declining to find a constitutional requirement to have a judicial-type procedure when a claim of incompetence at the time of execution is raised).

240 Id.

241 See Bloche, Psychiatry and Capital Punishment, supra note 126, at 307.

242 See FLA. STAT. [section] 922.07 (1983) (stating that the governor may act upon recommendations of psychiatrists).

243 Bloche, Psychiatry and Capital Punishment, supra note 126, at 307.

244 Id.

245 See id. at 309..

246 See Ford v. Wainwright, 477 U.S. 399, 413-16 (1986) (holding that prisoner must be able to offer evidence, cross-examine state's experts, and seek judicial review of fact-finding proceedings).

247 Id. at 418.

248 Bloche, Psychiatry and Capital Punishment, supra note 126, at 311-16.

249 See infra notes and accompanying text.

250 Bloche, Psychiatry and Capital Punishment, supra note 126, at 311-12.

251 Id. at 316-17.

252 Singleton v. Norris, 319 F.3d 1018 (8th Cir. 2003) (en banc) (holding that it is constitutionally permissible to forcefully medicate a prisoner in order to restore competency for execution); United States v. Sell, 282 F.3d 560 (8th Cir. 2002)

(holding that it is constitutionally permissible to forcefully medicate a prisoner in order to restore competency to stand trial).

253   504 U.S. 127 (1992).

254   Id. at 129-31.

255   See id. at 138 ("[T]he record contains no finding that might support a conclusion that administration of antipsychotic medication was necessary to accomplish an essential state policy ..."). The decision on this issue was reserved for another day. See id. at 135 ("[T]he State might have been able to justify medically appropriate, involuntary treatment with the drug by establishing that it could not obtain an adjudication of Riggins' guilt or innocence by using less intrusive means.") The Court may address it this Term in Sell v. United States, 123 S. Ct. 512 (2002) (order granting certiorari). 256 Riggins, 540 U.S. at 135.

257   Id.

258   Necessity would imply that there is no other choice. Medical appropriateness may simply mean that the treatment is one generally acceptable for a given condition and is not futile or one which is more detrimental than beneficent to the patient's health.

259   Id. at 138.

260   Sell v. United States, 123 S. Ct. 512 (2002) (order granting certiorari).

261   United States v. Sell, 282 F.3d 560 (8th Cir. 2002).

262   Id.

263   Id. at 568.

264   Id. at 563.

265   Id. at 568-70.

266   United States v. Sell, 282 F.3d at 570-71.

267   Id. at 568. The court only dealt with the Government's interest in bringing the defendant to trial and found that interest alone to be sufficient. See 282 F.3d at 568.

268   Id. Again, the court seems to assume that the measure of

"appropriateness" is simply efficacy; a proposition that is quite dubious from the viewpoint of medical ethics. See Part V, infra.

269   Singleton v. Norris, 319 F.3d 1018 (8th Cir. 2003) (en banc).

270   Id.

271   Id. at 1026.

272   Id. at 1036-37 (Jeaney, J., dissenting).

273   See, e.g., David A. Rothstein, M.D., Letter to the Editor, 20 Newsl. Am. Acad. Psychiatry & L. 111, 112 (1995). See also infra, Part V.A.

274   "Medical" in a sense that the NGRI acquitted are treated as any other patient confined to a mental institution would be. Although, obviously the acquitted are in the hospital involuntarily, their medical regimen does not depend on their status. In this sense, psychiatrists do not act as extensors of the penal system whose primary purpose is to advance penalogical interests, but instead as physicians who care for the ill.

275   See, e.g., 18 U.S.C. [section] 4243; MODEL PENAL CODE [section] 4.08(1).

276   LAFAVE, supra note 8, at 383. Nonetheless, commitment usually follows even in permissive jurisdictions. See GOLDSTEIN, supra note 8, at 145.

277   See supra, notes 45-46 and accompanying text.

278   See infra, notes 275-78 and accompanying text.

279   See supra, notes 15-47 and accompanying text.

280   See supra, notes 86-125 and accompanying text.

281   See supra, note 87 and accompanying text.

282   See supra, note 88 and accompanying text.

283   See supra, notes 17-47 and accompanying text.

284   SHELDON GLUECK, MENTAL DISORDER AND THE CRIMINAL LAW 392-93 (1925) ("before 1800, in England, and in most jurisdictions in this country, if an accused person was found to be irresponsible by reason of insanity he was forthwith

acquitted, and no special order looking to his safety or that of society was made".)

285   Abraham L. Halpern, The Insanity Verdict, The Psychopath, And Post-Acquittal Confinement, 24 PAC. L.J. 1125, 1129 (1993).

286   Id.

287   Id.

288   Id.

289   Id.

290   GLUECK, supra note 251, at 392-93.

291   Criminal Lunatics Act of 1800, 40 Geo. 3, c. 94 (1800).

292   The term "until His Majesty's pleasure be known" is the very definition of indefinite confinement.

293   The Act covered all felony NGRI acquittals, not just the serious ones. Criminal Lunatics Act of 1800, 40 Geo. 3, c. 94 (1800) ("[U]pon the trial of any person charged with treason, murder or felony ...")

294   See supra, notes 60-75 and accompanying text.

295   Halpern, supra notes 252, at 1132.

296   See id. at n.27 ("Ordinary lunatics at that time were sent to Bethlem Hospital, where the supervision was not particularly strict; and if Hadfield were to escape he would probably take another shot at the King") (quoting Ralph Partridge, Broadmoor 1 (1953)).

297   ROGER SMITH, TRIAL BY MEDICINE: INSANITY AND RESPONSIBILITY IN VICTORIAN TRIALS 23 (1981).

298   For example, Maryland allowed "mental defectives" (not the NGRI acquitted, but instead convicted individuals who were deemed to be "mentally defective") to be confined to Patuxent State Institution, for indefinite secure confinement. See State v. McCray, 297 A.2d 265, 268 (Md. 1972) (describing some of the restrictions in Patuxent).

299   See Munro, supra note 4, at 15-16 (For example,"[t]he death penalty for murder, normally mandatory in such cases, was not applied in cases where the offender was shown to be

insane at the time of the crime, even when the victim was one of the offender's own parents. An exception to this rule of clemency was made, however, if the victim was one of the grandparents. The death penalty was applied also in the case of multiple homicides by the insane").

300   Id. at 15.

301   Id.

302   Id.

303   Id.

304   Id.

305   See supra text accompanying notes 241-42.

306   See, e.g., 18 U.S.C. [section] 4243(e) ("[T]he Attorney General shall hospitalize the person for treatment in a suitable facility ...") (emphasis added).

307   See, e.g., Kansas v. Hendricks, 521 U.S. 346, 360-66 (1997) (noting that "under the appropriate circumstances and when accompanied by proper procedures, incapacitation [as opposed to treatment] may be a legitimate end of the civil law"); Jones v. United States, 463 U.S. 354, 368 (1983) (noting that "the purpose of commitment following an insanity acquittal ... is to treat the individual's mental illness and protect him and society from his potential dangerousness") (emphasis added).

308   HALPERN, supra note 252, at 1134.

309   Id.

310   850 F.2d 231 (5th Cir. 1988).

311   See id. at 235 (One of the physicians testified that sanity can be feigned, albeit he qualified that by stating it is unlikely that such feigning can go on for more than a few hours. The trial court, relying on the testimony of that physician, declined to release Francois anyway).

312   See supra text accompanying note 137.

313   Id.

314   Id.

315   Id.

316   For a description of the Soviet system see M. Gregg Bloche, Law, Theory and Politics: The Dilemma of Soviet Psychiatry, 11 YALE J. INT'L. L. 297 (1986) (hereinafter Soviet Psychiatry).

317   For a description of the People's Republic of China's system see MUNRO, supra note 4.

318   The Russian Federation inherited its system from the former Soviet Union and did not significantly change it. Russia recently adopted a new Criminal Procedural Code in 2001, although it did not take effect until July 1, 2002. Prior to that the Russian Federation used the old Soviet Criminal Procedure Code of 1960. Federal'nyi Zakon No. 177-FZ 12/18/2001, Ross. Gazeta 12/22/2001.

319   See id. at n.95. Procuracy (Prokuratura) is a State organ (both in the USSR and RF) separate from the Ministry of Justice that is responsible for bringing prosecutions, investigating cases, and ensuing compliance with the law.

320   See BLOCHE, supra note 283, at 318.

321   Id. at 318.

322   Id. at 323. Although at first glance this may be seen as subtracting from the authority of the experts conducting the examination, it does not have to be. In the United States experts often follow guidelines published by the Group for Advancement of Psychiatry, and follow the diagnostic pattern based on the latest edition of the Diagnostic and Statistical Manual of Mental Disorders.

323   Id. at 319.

324   See id. at 320-23 (discussing the role of value preferences).

325   Id.

326   Id.

327   Id.

328   Id.

329   See id. at 319. (The Court reviews the psychiatrists' finding as to whether the defendant is responsible for his conduct. Of course, as stated above, such review is quite perfunctory.)

330   Id. at 318. (noting that "psychiatric examiners appointed by investigators and courts are officially viewed as impartial and

objective; thus defense consultation with experts is deemed unnecessary.")

331 See supra text accompanying notes 193-194.

332 See generally BLOCHE, supra note 283.

333 See generally MUNRO, supra note 4.

334 See Edmund D. Pellegrino, Physician's Dilemma of Divided Loyalty, 16 INT'L. J. L. & PSYCHIATRY 371, 373 (1993).

335 See infra notes 307-35 and the accompanying text.

336 See, e.g., GOLDSTEIN, supra note 8, at 122; BLOCHE, supra note 283, at 320-23.

337 Any psychiatrist projects his views on the problem before him, but an "independent one" is free from the threat of probing and/or impeaching questions or counter testimony. Thus, an "independent" expert is not checked by anything.

338 Cf. BLOCHE, supra note 283, at 318. (noting that either the court or the Procuracy appoint the "experts," and, being agents of the repressive state, they presumably have little interest in having dissident's view bolstered.)

339 See Michael R. Gordon, Russian Troops in Chechnya Find Little Quiet on the Southern Front, N.Y. TIMES, Jan. 10, 2000, at A1.

340 http://www.gazeta.ru/2002/01/15/sudzabylopol.shtml (last visited Apr. 14, 2003).

341 UK RF [section] 286(1).

342 UK RF [section] 126.

343 UK RF [section] 131.

344 http://www.rambler.ru/db/news/msg.html?mid=3241998&s=11 (last visited Apr. 14, 2003); see also http://www.gazeta.ru/2002/05/16/budanovpsiho.shtml (stating that forensic examination concluded that genital bruising was post-mortem) (last visited Apr. 14, 2003).

345 UK RF [section] 105(2), http://www.gazeta.ru/2002/05/13/kakrazvivalo.shtml.

346 http://www.gazeta.ru/2002/01/15/sudzabylopol.shtml (last visited Apr. 14, 2003).

347   See UK RF [section] 216. As a federal officer, Budanov had the authority to detain and interrogate suspected terrorists. He claimed that during interrogation Ms. Kungaeva attacked him and he responded disproportionally. This behavior is "clearly beyond official powers," and therefore would subject Budanov to prosecution for violating UK RF [section] 216. On the issue of being attacked see http://www.gazeta.ru/2002/05/13/kakrazvivalo.shtml (last visited Apr. 14, 2003).

348   "Nevmeniaem" is often translated as "criminally irresponsible," although this translation does not give full appreciation of the term's meaning. In all its fullness, the term encompasses lack of criminal responsibility, legal insanity, and lack of social awareness of one's actions. Indeed, one of the colloquial translations of "nevmeniaem" is "beside oneself." OXFORD RUSSIAN-ENGLISH DICTIONARY 267 (1994).

349   http://www.rambler.ru/db/news/msg.html?mid=3242564&s=11 (last visited Apr. 14, 2003); see also Patrick Tyler, Police in Chechnya Accuse Russia's Troops of Murder, N.Y. TIMES, Jan. 25, 2002, at A1 (stating that military officials "demand[ed] ... psychiatric evaluations ... to determine whether Colonel Budanov was temporarily insane").

350   See Michael R. Gordon, Russian Official Tries to Ensure Rights in Chechnya, N.Y. TIMES, May 7, 2000, at A6 (noting that "most Russian officials reject Western human rights complaints as a plot to blacken the nation's image").

351   http://www.rambler.ru/db/news/msg.html?mid=3241925&s=15 (last visited Apr. 14, 2003).

352   See, e.g., http://www.rambler.ru/db/news/msg.html?mid=3241891&s=11 (President of the Buryat Republic claims that Budanov may have been a victim of a Chechen plot) (last visited Apr. 14, 2003); http://www.rambler.ru/db/news/msg.html?mid=1559218&s=2 (Cossacks and former commander of troops in Chechnya support Budanov. General Shamilov claimed that the Budanov is accused only because of "ideological intervention of the West against Russia.") (last visited Apr. 14, 2003); http://www.rambler.ru/db/news/msg.html?mid=3242284&s=11 (Up to 50% of Russians believe

that Budanov is not guilty of murder) (last visited Apr. 14, 2003).

353   http://www.rambler.ru/db/news/msg.html?mid=1230830&s=2 (last visited Apr. 14, 2003)

354   http://www.gazeta.ru/2002/12/31/budanovprizn.shtml (last visited Apr. 14, 2003).

355   See   http://www.rambler.ru/db/news/msg.html?mid=2355527&s=9 (mentioning second evaluation) (last visited Apr. 14, 2003).

356   See id. (Judge refusing to reveal the results of the evaluation) (last visited Apr. 14, 2003).

357   http://www.rambler.ru/db/news/msg.html?mid=3242565&s=11 (last visited Apr. 14, 2003).

358   Id.

359   http://www.rambler.ru/db/news/msg.html?mid=1944662&s=10 (last visited Apr. 14, 2003).

360   Russian law provides for the victim or his family to be a part of a criminal prosecution. Indeed, even if the state prosecution and defense are satisfied with the outcome of the case, the victim's attorney can still appeal. UK RF [section] 45.

361   http://www.rambler.ru/db/news/msg.html?mid=2634075&s=10 (last visited Apr. 14, 2003).

362   Id.

363   http://www.rambler.ru/db/news/msg.html?mid=3051705&s=11 (last visited Apr. 14, 2003).

364   http://www.rambler.ru/db/news/msg.html?mid=3051704&s=11 (last visited Apr. 14, 2003).

365   http://www.rambler.ru/db/news/msg.html?mid=3090899&s=11 (The court characterized the psychiatric conclusion merely as "scientifically sound" and based on such finding declared Col. Budanov was "nevmeniaem" at the time of the crime.) (last visited Apr. 14, 2003).

366   On February 28th, 2003, the Military Collegium of the Supreme Court of Russian Federation set aside the decision of the lower court as procedurally erroneous, and remanded

the case back to that court. It further ordered that the case be tried before a different panel of judges. Michael Wines, Russia Orders a New Trial In Chechnya Murder Case, N.Y. TIMES, Mar. 1, 2003 at A4.

367   See Michael Wines, Chechens Seize Moscow Theater, Taking as Many as 600 Hostages, N.Y. TIMES, Oct. 24, 2002, at A1; Michael Wines, Russia Recaptures Theater After Chechen Rebel Group Begins to Execute Hostages, N.Y. TIMES, Oct. 26, 2002, at A1. The fourth evaluation was conducted sometime between July 21, 2002 (the date when Budanov was sent from Rostov-on-Don, where he was tried, to Moscow, where he was evaluated) and September 29, 2002 (when the evaluation ended), http://www.rambler.ru/db/news/msg.html?mid=2826637&s=10 (last visited Apr. 14, 2003). Although the evaluation was completed September 29, the report was not submitted until November, creating the possibility that the hostage situation in Moscow influenced the examiners' findings. No such accusations are being levied, but the mere possibility is quite troubling, http://www.rambler.ru/db/   news/msg.html?mid=3251957&s=2 (stating that on November 18, 2002 all documents relating to the evaluation were completed and forwarded to the court) (last visited Apr. 14, 2003).

368   See, e.g., Paul Appelbaum, Psychiatric Ethics in the Courtroom, 12 BULL. AM. ACAD. PSYCHIATRY & L. 225 (1984).

369   Id.

370   Id.

371   See David A. Rothstein, M.D., Psychiatrists' Involvement in Executions: Arriving at an Official Position, 20 NEWSLETTER AM. ACAD. PSYCHIATRY & L. 15, 17 (1995) ("anyone acting in a capacity that requires a psychiatrist's education, judgment, and experience is, in that role, practicing psychiatry.") If someone is practicing psychiatry, it then follows, that one is acting as a physician. If that is so, one must assume all the duties and moral obligations of a physician.

372   This principle is derived from the Hippocratic Oath that states, in part "I will prescribe regimen for the good of my patients according to my ability and my judgment and never do harm

to anyone." STEADMAN'S MED. DICTIONARY 799 (26th ed.) (1995).

373   The idea that a patient must consent to treatment derives from the Kantian notion that a person can never be a means to an end. If treatment is undertaken without consent, a person is used as a means towards the end of better health. In order for the person to be the end, not merely a means to an end, he must want to participate in a given activity, i.e., he must consent. The notion of consent also derives in part from the common law of battery. See Cruzan ex rel. Cruzan v. Director, Missouri Dept. of Health, 497 U.S. 261, 269 (1990).

374   Medically appropriate here means efficacious and within accepted medical practice.

375   There may be a "satisfaction" benefit to a patient who requests the procedure as a result of having his wishes fulfilled. This will be discussed shortly.

376   See Part V.A.2.

377   Id.

378   See Part V.A.2.

379   See PHYSICIAN'S DESK REFERENCE 2284 (56th ed.) (2002).

380   See BLOCHE, supra note 126, at 316-19.

381   For example hair loss results from chemotherapy, and a loss of limb results from amputation due to gangrene

382   As suggested below, the mere fact that clinical benefits outweigh the clinical harms is not a blanket license to act in the face of the patient's disagreement with that assessment.

383   See Rothstein, supra note 338 and accompanying text.

384   Here incarceration is limited strictly to criminal confinement.

385   See, e.g., Mafia A. Morrison, Changing Perceptions of Mental Illness and the Emergence of Expansive Mental Health Parity Legislation, 45 S.D.L. REV. 8, 8-9 (2000).

386   This does not necessarily imply that it is unethical for a physician to cause a death of an ill individual, as in for example assisted suicide. Irrespective of how one chooses to think about the issue of assisted suicide, it has to be conceded that

causing a death of a healthy individual through the use of medical knowledge is ethically unacceptable.

387   See generally Alan H. Goldman, The Refutation of Medical Paternalism, THE MORAL FOUNDATIONS OF PROFESSIONAL ETHICS.

388   Id.

389   Id.

390   It does not follow that the physician always must act in accordance with patient's wishes, though. A patient may desire an intervention that does not satisfy the "no harm" analysis. In other words, a physician is not required to perform a procedure simply because the patient so desires, but is required to abstain from performing it if the patient refuses it.

391   See AMERICAN MEDICAL ASSOCIATION POLICY COMPENDIUM, Informed Consent, (Opinion of Council on Ethical and Judicial Affairs, E-8.08, 1981).

392   Certain antipsychotics can cause tardive dyskenesia, a permanent movement disorder. PHYSICIAN'S DESK REFERENCE 2535 (56th ed.) (2002).

393   Of course, neither a child, nor a person with such a low IQ score as to be considered incompetent, will most likely be tried. Nor can these individuals be medicated into competence, so treatment questions arise only in the context of civil commitment.

394   The word "reasonably" is purposefully omitted. Just because a person makes a decision that given all the information available is "unreasonable" (e.g., refusing a blood transfusion when such transfusion is medically necessary) does not automatically mean that a person could not understand the information. Only a person who cannot understand the information should be deemed unable to give or withhold consent; not merely a person who makes decisions different from those that a "reasonable man" would make under similar circumstances.

395   When a patient's values/wishes are known, these wishes must be considered to be in the patient's "best interests"

when the patient's values/wishes are not known, the choice that another person (possibly the physician himself, if there are no relatives or others close to the patient to consult with) would make in a similar situation for himself become what would be in the patient's "best interests." It is of course preferable that the physician try to elucidate whenever possible the wishes and values of the patient in question, instead of making a decision on his own.

396   See In re Quinlan, 355 A.2d 647 (N.J. 1976) (holding that when a person cannot give consent a substitute judgment that takes account of the best interests of the patient must be used); see also In re Conroy, 486 A.2d 1209 (N.J. 1985) (holding that patient's own wishes if expressed while competent should predominate when making substituted judgment).

397   This determination is not to be made by a physician, but by appropriate regulatory agencies. These agencies can institute reporting requirements for infectious disease, and then deal with the situation if the individual refuses treatment.

398   Saying that individual's rights are diminished does not mean, ipso facto, that he must undergo treatment. Rather, it is an observation that when an individual presents a threat to society, he is faced with a choice of being treated or being put in such situation where he cannot threaten others. The choice nonetheless is his.

399   See supra text accompanying note 339.

400   STEADMAN'S MED. DICTIONARY 799 (26th ed.) (1995) (text of Hippocratic Oath, "I will preserve the purity of my life and my art.").

401   See Part V.A.1.

402   See supra, accompanying notes 131-34; see also HAGEN, supra note 139.

403   LAFAVE, supra, note 8, at 378; see also supra text accompanying note 133.

404   The American Psychiatric Association, for example, condemned this practice, stating that "[t]he ability of psychiatrists or any other professionals to reliably predict future violence is

unproved." AMERICAN PSYCHIATRIC ASSOCIATION, CLINICAL ASPECTS OF THE VIOLENT INDIVIDUAL 30 (1974). Studies have shown that psychiatrists are right in their predictions roughly 1/3 of the time, an abysmal record by any standards (after all, pure guessing would produce right answers roughly 50% of the time). The false positive rate was even higher, 80%. See JOHN MONAHAN, PREDICTING VIOLENT BEHAVIOR: AN ASSESSMENT OF CLINICAL TECHNIQUES 64-67 (1981). Despite these studies, psychiatrists continue to give and courts continue to use such testimony. See Mark David Albertson, Can Violence Be Predicted? Future Dangerousness: The Testimony of Experts in Capital Cases, 3-WTR CRIM. JUST. 18, 19 (1989).

405   LAFAVE, supra, note 8, at 378; see also State v. McCann, 47 S.W.2d 95 (Mo. 1932).

406   See Sundby, supra, note 82; see also State v. Evans, 523 A.2d 1306 (Conn. 1987); Montano v. State, 468 N.E.2d 1042 (Ind. 1984); Ice v. Commonwealth, 667 S.W.2d 671 (Ky. 1984); Commonwealth v. Tyson, 402 A.2d 995 (Pa. 1979); see also supra text accompanying note 187.

407   Rothstein, supra, note 338.

408   One assumes that during the evaluation a psychiatrist is acting professionally, and that he is practicing good psychiatry.

409   Although this section speaks in terms of competency to stand trial, everything said applies with equal if not greater force to the situation where competency to be executed is at issue.

410   Because no harm come from the evaluation itself, a psychiatrist is not obligated to completely withdraw from the process. As any other physician, he can observe the patient, and share his observations with others (within the legal limits of the patient's right to confidentiality).

411   See supra notes 175-188 and accompanying text.

412   The expert testifying for the defendant is usually given more credence by the court than the prosecution expert. See LAFAVE, supra note 8, at 372; Weihofen, supra note 13, at 967-68.

413   Id.

414   If the psychiatrist is hired by the defense, he may assume that prison ranks lower than an NGRI acquittal on the defendant's value-preference scale. If the psychiatrist is hired by the prosecution, he too is aware of the same value-scale, yet acts contrary to it.

415   See supra notes 16-17 and the accompanying text.

416   Alternatively, it can be argued that while the psychiatrist for the prosecution cannot testify on moral issues under the "no harm" principle, the psychiatrist for the defense cannot testify on these issues under the "professionalism" principle. (Of course, the prosecution's psychiatrist is also constrained by the "professionalism" principle, but there is no need to reach it as the "no harm" principle comes first).

417   There is a separate problem with the "battle of the experts," namely that such spectacles demean medicine as a profession because they suggest that there is no objective truth or criteria in the field of psychiatry. A corollary of the above problem is disillusioned juries ignoring psychiatric testimony altogether, thus defeating the very purpose behind "expert witnesses." See Part III, supra. Thus, "battles of the experts," especially on issues that are not grounded in medical science are to be avoided on the "professionalism" principle. They may be avoided by using independent panels, but it is by no means the only way, and certainly not an acceptable one, if not coupled with the limitations on testimony previously discussed in this article.

418   An individual incompetent to stand trial may be competent to refuse medication, but in that case the dilemma is easier because consent can be given or withheld. The issue here is what to do with those incompetent to stand trial (be executed) and give consent to medical treatment.

419   See Part V.A.2.

420   AMERICAN MEDICAL ASSOCIATION POLICY COMPENDIUM, Capital Punishment (Opinion of Council on Ethical and Judicial Affairs, E-2.06, 1980, updated 1992, 1994, 1995, 1998, 1999, 2000).

421   Of course the doctor is not the one who should be making the decision, but rather a guardian for that patient. The

guardian often is the state, whose interests may be contrary to the patient's (e.g., execution). A physician nonetheless can medicate such a patient provided that death is not an immediate result of such medication. A physician may medicate the patient only to a point where the patient can decide for himself whether or not to continue with the treatment.

422   See Part V.A.2 (stating that in situations where an individual is dangerous to society, and no other method to control dangerousness exists, a patient can be mediated without his consent.) This is however, a rare and extreme case.

423   See supra notes 275-79 and the accompanying text.

424   The behavior also violates the "professionalism" principle, because whenever psychiatrists act as merely a penalogical tool, they demean the profession. Although the "professionalism" principle is violated, as discussed above, there is no need to reach it. See supra, note 382.

425   See Bloche, supra note 126, at 323-37; see also Richard J. Bonnie, The Death Penalty: When Doctors Must Say No, 305 BRIT. MED. J. 381 (1982); Richard J. Bonnie, Healing-Killing Conflicts: Medical Ethics and the Death Penalty, 20 HASTINGS CENTER REP. 12, 13 (1990)

426   See Part V.B.1.

427   Id.

428   Granted, in most instances NGRI acquitted are civilly confined. See infra, notes 246-77 and the accompanying text. However, the possibility does exist that such release will occur.

429   See supra, notes 113-14 and the accompanying text.

430   The very definition of a valid scientific experiment is that it is reproducible. If one cannot come to the same result using the same data, the experiment is not considered valid.

431   Ford v. Wainwright, 477 U.S. 399 (1986).

432   It is not for this article to debate whether all, some or none of these claims of incompetence are genuine. What this article does suggest that given the stakes, it is possible and indeed desirable (from the point of view of the condemned)

to attempt to manipulate the system, and enlist help of the psychiatrist in the process.

433 See Bloche, Psychiatry and Capital Punishment, supra note 126, at 311-16.

434 Id. at 305-10.

435 Id. at 305.

436 Id. at 306.

437 Id.

438 Id. Although competency for execution may not be the same as competency to stand trial, given the very low threshold for the former, one is likely to satisfy it if one is competent to stand trial. See Ford v. Wainwright, 477 U.S. 399, 421 (Powell, J., concurring) (stating that one is competent for execution if one has "awareness of the penalty's existence and purpose"). It seems that this is a less demanding standard then competency for trial where one needs to be not only aware of the proceedings, but be able to understand them.

439 Bloche, Psychiatry and Capital Punishment, supra note 126, at 306.

440 Id.

441 Id. This is not to say that these procedures met the requirements later announced in Ford. Nonetheless, the states did undertake a separate evaluation of the condemned.

442 The actual procedural requirements are quite unclear. Although Ford v. Wainwright, did hold that executing the incompetent is not constitutionally permissible, and required that the prisoner be heard on the issue, the parameters of the hearing are unclear. See LAFAVE, supra note 8, at 362.

443 Bloche, Psychiatry and Capital Punishment, supra note 126, at 306.

444 477 U.S. 399.

445 See, e.g., Solesbee v. Balkcom, 339 U.S. 9, 11-12 (1950) (declining to find a constitutional requirement to have a judicial-type procedure when a claim of incompetence at the time of execution is raised).

446 Id.

447 See Bloche, Psychiatry and Capital Punishment, supra note 126, at 307.

448 See FLA. STAT. [section] 922.07 (1983) (stating that the governor may act upon recommendations of psychiatrists).

449 Bloche, Psychiatry and Capital Punishment, supra note 126, at 307.

450 Id.

451 See id. at 309.

452 See Ford v. Wainwright, 477 U.S. 399, 413-16 (1986) (holding that prisoner must be able to offer evidence, cross-examine state's experts, and seek judicial review of fact-finding proceedings).

453 Id. at 418.

454 Bloche, Psychiatry and Capital Punishment, supra note 126, at 311-16.

455 See infra notes and accompanying text.

456 Bloche, Psychiatry and Capital Punishment, supra note 126, at 311-12.

457 Id. at 316-17.

458 Singleton v. Norris, 319 F.3d 1018 (8th Cir. 2003) (en banc) (holding that it is constitutionally permissible to forcefully medicate a prisoner in order to restore competency for execution); United States v. Sell, 282 F.3d 560 (8th Cir. 2002) (holding that it is constitutionally permissible to forcefully medicate a prisoner in order to restore competency to stand trial).